GET
WEALTHY
FOR
SURE™

GET
WEALTHY
FOR
SURE™

The #1 Financial Strategy For Business
Owners To Multiply Wealth Predictably

M.C. LAUBSCHER

M.C. Laubscher
mc@mclaubscher.com
https://producerswealth.com/

Get Wealthy For Sure™, M.C. Laubscher —1st ed.

DEDICATION

This book is dedicated to R. Nelson Nash, thank you for teaching me how to think like a bank, act like a bank, and be my own bank.

CONTENTS

PRAISE FOR M.C. LAUBSCHER

"M.C. Laubscher is a distinguished authority in the realm of personal finance, particularly with the Infinite Banking Concept. His profound understanding and practical application of becoming your own banker are truly transformative. M.C. embodies the principles he advocates, offering a blend of profound wisdom, real-world experience, and unwavering commitment. He excels not only in establishing robust personal banking systems but also in his role as a mentor, guiding and inspiring individuals to take control of their financial future. His dedication to education and his willingness to share his journey make him a genuine beacon for anyone aspiring to master their financial destiny."
Dave Wolcott, Pantheon Investments

"A few years ago, I attended the Mid-Atlantic Conference and heard M.C. speak about collateralization. His innovative approach resonated deeply, as my own strategy lacked a cohesive plan. M.C.'s ability to translate complex topics like family offices and generational wealth planning – strategies typically reserved for the ultra-wealthy – into actionable steps for someone like me was truly eye-opening. By implementing the action steps outlined in his Aligned Capital Strategy, I've not only discovered powerful financial tools but also gained the confidence to use them and significantly improve my financial future."

Denis Shapiro, SIH Capital Group

"Having worked closely with MC Laubscher, I can confidently affirm his position as one of the foremost authorities on implementing the Infinite Banking Concept strategy for business owners and investors. Hailing from South Africa, MC brings a unique perspective shaped by witnessing economic downturns and the unpreparedness of many in the face of such crises.

MC's guidance goes beyond mere establishment; he mentors individuals, helping them become their own bank and navigate the financial landscape with confidence. What truly sets MC apart is his commitment to practicing what he preaches. Drawing from his own experiences, he generously shares insights into his personal banking system, continually educating others and imparting valuable lessons learned from his journey.

If you're seeking to take control of your financial future in the wake of uncertain economic times, MC Laubscher's expertise is unparalleled. His mentorship will not only empower you to implement the Infinite Banking Concept but also equip you with the knowledge and resilience needed to thrive in any economic environment."

Kent Kiess, KC Investments

"MC Laubscher has been a tremendous resource for my business. He's offered tremendous educational content and has helped me set up my financial fortress for the long term. I now have 2 policies with MC and as more business growth and income is produced, we will continue to open policies for my family's future."

Cassidy Burns, BPG Holdings

"MC Laubscher is a leading authority in the Infinite Banking Concept, offering unparalleled mentorship to business owners and investors. He excels not only in teaching the principles of managing one's own banking system but also in applying these strategies in his own life, providing real-world insights. MC's continuous support and sharing of his personal financial journey make him a valuable guide towards achieving financial independence."

Saket Jain, Impact Wealth Builders & Migrate 2 Wealth

"I was introduced to the Infinite Banking Concept during a Real Estate conference where M.C. was a featured speaker. Since that day, "IBC" has become the foundation of our family's journey towards achieving Wealth, Freedom, and a lasting Legacy. M.C. has been with us at each phase and each accomplished milestone providing us with invaluable guidance as our trusted advisor. "Get Wealthy For Sure™" is an investment in yourself, your family, and your future legacy."

Karl Schnitzer, entrepreneur and investor

'The Infinite Banking Concept can be a daunting concept to the newcomer as it is not taught in conventional circles. However, conventional thinking doesn't build real wealth or lead you down the path to financial independence.

MCs real gift is not just his mastery of the concept or ability to create these uniquely structured policies where he excels is in breaking this concept down to easily understandable concepts that both the layman and expert can understand.

Likewise, MC has endless real-world examples of how individuals are utilizing infinite banking to both protect and grow their hard-earned dollars.

MCs passion for helping people achieve financial freedom shines brightly in all of his teachings, writings, and podcasts.'
Dan Nicastro, real estate investor

"MC spent a ton of time with my wife and I to ensure we understood the whole life strategy. Fast forward to today, we have two policies and are eager to get more. Thanks again for the excellent service."
Hunter Thompson, Asym Capital

"We vividly remember the first time we met M.C. Laubscher. We heard him on a popular podcast, and we were instantly captivated by his unique approach to capital and business.

M.C. explained that growing your financial capital isn't just about focusing on the money. It's about nurturing your human and relationship capital first. The more you develop these areas, the more your financial capital will grow. It was an eye-opener, and it's been the driving force behind our work for the past five years.

M.C. has helped us manage our cashflow better, become more cash flow efficient, and help us to create our own banking system through the Infinite Banking Concept. These strategies have been a game-changer for us and our family, and continue to be a game-changer on our wealth-building journey."

Josh & Melanie McCallen, Accountable Equity,
Business Owners & Investors

"M.C. Laubscher is a passionate, focused, and driven person. Not only does he have abundant experience in IBC, but he also understands clients' needs and expectations, giving genuine advice and planning. His extensive knowledge and broad network further enable him to provide useful and down-to-earth strategies. He is absolutely the one to go for building personal wealth."

Jenny Yeh, investor

"MC and his work with Producers Wealth has been a game changer for me and my family. MC is a leader in the teachings of Infinite Banking and how to use whole life insurance to take back the banking function in your life and control your legacy and wealth transfer. Before I started to listen to MC I had no idea about the concept of Infinite Banking but once I gathered the courage to reach out, MC introduced me to a new way of thinking when it comes to financing investments and business ventures. In just a few short years I have been able to not only grow significant cash value in a whole life policy, but I have been able to expand my real estate portfolio beyond residential, into commercial, as well as provide financing for my own business expansion. The growth has been exponential. Plus I am building wealth to transfer to my children and grandchildren but perhaps more importantly, I have been able to build a system that I am teaching to them that will leave a legacy for many generations to come."

Todd Concienne, business owner and investor

"MC practices what he preaches. After looking at several different insurance policies at many different companies, MC immediately stood out as an independent agent and offered up several options that were far superior to what I had previously seen. I would highly recommend MC to anyone looking to implement IBC, especially real estate investors looking to stay away from volatile securities."

Al Meger, real estate broker

"I've followed MC for many years and have implemented some of the infinite banking cashflow strategies he covers. MC is a thought leader in the cashflow investing space and has interviewed the very best out there. Thank you MC for pulling together your incredible insights together!"

Michael Hakoun, investor

"Working with M.C. Laubscher on navigating the Infinite Banking Concept (IBC) has been a game-changer in my investment journey. What sets M.C. apart isn't just his mastery of IBC, but his knack for making complex strategies accessible for someone like me, who's always on the go and doesn't have the luxury of diving deep into financial minutiae. He's been more than an advisor; he's been a mentor who's patiently guided me through setting up and optimizing my policy, ensuring I'm not just following steps but truly understanding each move. His practical advice, drawn from real-life use of his own system, has demystified the banking concept, allowing me to secure and grow my investments, even in unpredictable markets. It's rare to find someone who not only 'talks the talk' but also 'walks the walk' with such integrity and passion. M.C. has genuinely enhanced my financial well-being and confidence, making a tangible difference in how I view and manage my financial future."

Rayn Murray, business owner and investor

"If you are looking to create generation wealth and a family legacy then MC Laubscher is the guy to want to listen to. My family and I have had the honor and privilege to work with MC for many years now. His information on IBC (Infinite Banking System) has guided us in every financial decision we have made from purchasing investment properties to starting businesses and accredited investments.

We have several IBC accounts with MC and will get several more in the future. Thank you MC for your guidance and mentorship. Can't wait to have our children read the book so they can pass on generational wealth. "

Sean Kiess, business owner and investor

"M.C. tailored the finest financial toolkit for us to weather storms while taking advantage of massive opportunities. As the world continued its accelerated meltdown over the past several years, our IBC policies gave us peace of mind while we experienced an unplanned surgery. Shortly thereafter, these same policies enabled us to purchase our dream property that began our off-grid homestead adventure. His mentorship is second to none. His knowledge is priceless. His system is flexible. The seed M.C. sows germinates into family legacies. The season is now and, through Producers Wealth, the soil is ever so fertile."

James & Ashley Strand, Strand Farm, LLC (YouTube)

"MC Laubscher is a renowned expert in the Infinite Banking Concept and has helped countless individuals and businesses apply the correct strategy for their situation. There are only a handful of people that advise high net worth families on setting up insurance policies and they generally do not provide service to the public. MC is a rare gem in that he will help you set up your Infinite Banking System and then be a mentor as you grow. I am blessed to have MC in my rolodex of advisors."

Dan Albershardt, Business Owner

INTRODUCTION

As a business owner, you know the meaning of the phrase "opportunity cost" all too well.

For every decision you make, opportunity cost hangs in the balance. What if you take one path and lose the opportunity to make hundreds of thousands of dollars? What if your decision to pursue one marketing idea over the other costs you dozens of new clients?

The skill of a business owner lies in seeing opportunities where others do not.

Over your career, you've honed this skill and built a business that brings value to your niche... All because you saw an opportunity that someone else did not.

Now, your success has left you with excess capital. What do you do with this capital? Where would you warehouse it efficiently to protect and grow it?

What if I told you that the way you've been taught to financially plan by financial advisors is costing you millions in opportunity cost?

And what if I told you that you're missing out on the #1 financial strategy for business owners today?

Before you get scared off... Don't worry, this book isn't going to sell you some newfangled get-rich-quick strategy like buying a meme stock or investing in an NFT that looks like a cartoon monkey.

I'm going to share a strategy that wealthy business owners, including the Rockefellers, Walt Disney, and countless top CEOs of today, have been using for 170+ years to Get Wealthy For Sure™.

What does it mean to Get Wealthy For Sure™?

Sorry, but I can't tell you how to get rich quick. There's no way to get rich quick that's any likelier than winning the lottery (I hear you have a higher chance of being struck by lightning... And that most lottery winners die broke).

So if you want to get rich quick, feel free to put down this book, put on your lucky socks, and visit your local fortune teller to find out your next move.

But I can give you something better... I can tell you how to Get Wealthy For Sure™.

What does it mean to Get Wealthy For Sure™?

It means you're playing the long game. At the end of your life, you'll know that the wealth you worked hard to build all those years you spent creating your business will be preserved for generations of your family to come.

And along the way, you've enjoyed the power and freedom that this strategy gives you to grow your business, make investments, seize opportunities, and survive crises.

Meanwhile, you watch some of your competitors crumble because they were not able to survive crises and seize on opportunities during these crises.

The strategy I'm going to share gives you:

1. Clarity
2. Certainty
3. Predictability

You'll never again have to wonder if your investments will generate the returns you want... You'll know.

You'll never again have to wonder if you're investing your wealth in the right way... You'll know.

With clarity, certainty, and predictability, you can stop worrying about your finances and focus on doing what you do best: being a business owner.

But if you don't invest the time to learn about this strategy, you'll forever have to live with the fear that you're missing out on the single greatest investment strategy for business owners and losing millions of dollars in opportunity cost.

Do you want to live with that fear? I didn't think so.

Let's get started…

CHAPTER 1

Are You Betting On Yourself–Or Someone Else?

"The best bet you'll ever make is on yourself."

–Warren Buffett

You got where you are today because you bet on you.

You had a vision to start a business that would impact the world and give you control over your own destiny. You didn't wait for someone else to hand this opportunity to you… You bet on yourself and took the leap out of your career and into the new frontier of building a business from scratch.

Today, you're successful, but victory didn't happen overnight. Let's rewind and remember what it took to get here…

The first year of any business can be rough. You're trying to manage cashflow, build out infrastructure, hire the right employees, and so much more. Yes, you have a business, but because you're in the building phase, your business doesn't look good on a financial statement.

When you want to get loans or business credit cards, nobody wants to give you the time of day. The highest quality attorneys, tax accountants, and financial advisors won't take meetings with you because you don't fit their ideal client profile– yes, you're on your way to being the next game-changing entrepreneur in your niche, but according to the numbers, you look like a broke person with a dream.

But eventually, you climb out of the struggle period. Now, you're generating revenue, and the business is finally profitable. You bet on yourself and won!

You solved countless problems to get here, but soon, another problem begins to creep in...

As you generate revenue, you reinvest it in the business, and the business grows and grows, generating even more revenue, which you reinvest in the business... It's like a snowball rolling downhill and getting bigger as it gains momentum.

You now have the opposite of the problem you started with: you have too much money.

What do you do with all of the excess capital your business generates?

The dangerous part of this problem is that because you're successful, every financial planner wants to sit down with you and sell you a product. You may have dozens of voices in your ear, vying for you to be their next client, telling you that their way is the best way. Who should you believe? Out of the seemingly endless buffet of solutions, which is the right one?

Wealth has to reside and be warehoused somewhere…

Let's explore some of the most common places it can reside.

The Banks

Can't you just leave your money in the banks?

Right, the banks, where, under the Dodd-Frank Act[1] enacted in 2010, you're an unsecured creditor to the bank. Meaning once you put money in a bank account, it's not even yours anymore.

This legislation, which resulted from the financial crisis of 2008, was passed with the intent that there would never be a full-scale bailout again.

How safe are banks right now? Early in 2023, five banks went under[2]. By the end of 2023, you had ten banks downgraded by rating agencies and eleven banks placed on a watchlist[3].

People might say, "Well, sure, that sounds scary, but there's always FDIC insurance." But by the FDIC's own admission,

---

[1]   United States, Congress. Public Law 111-203, Dodd-Frank Wall Street Reform and Consumer Protection Act. *govinfo.gov,* July 21, 2010. *U.S. Government Printing Office.*

[2]   FDIC. "Failed Bank List." *FDIC.gov*, November 3, 2023

[3]   Rutledge, Ann. "The Big Three Are Downgrading Banks, But Are They In Bad Shape?" *Forbes*, August 28, 2023

they only have 2% of what they have insured in reserves[4]. They can't bail out your bank account.

Do you want to bet on the banks? I didn't think so…

Bonds

What about bonds? With bonds, you have the threat of counterparty risk. How solvent is the entity or government that's issuing the bond? None of them are solvent…

Interest rates for bonds are massive.

An interest rate spike can devalue your bond significantly. If you buy a bond of $100,000 at an interest rate of 2.5%, the bond will pay you $2,500. When interest rates go up significantly and move to 5%, the bond that you bought at 2.5% is now only worth $50,000 because a bond of $50,000 purchased with a 5% interest rate will pay out $2,500… The same as a $100,000 bond bought with a 2.5% interest rate…

Fun fact, 5 banks collapsed in 2023 because they bought bonds with reserves at low-interest rates, and then interest rates more than doubled.

Do you want to take the risk that interest rates will spike? In such a volatile economic environment where most bond issuers are bankrupt and interest rates fluctuate, only a gambler would take that bet.

---

[4]   Mitchell, Patrick. Memo the Board of Directors Re: Designated Reserve Ratio for 2024, FDIC. November 16, 2023.

Invest in the Market

As a successful business owner, you have dozens of financial planners telling you, "Your business is crushing it. Why don't you give me some of your money, and I'll invest it in stocks, bonds, and mutual funds so we can grow your wealth and diversify your portfolio?"

But what these financial planners don't say is that when you invest in stocks, bonds, mutual funds, ETFs, and other common investments, you're investing in *other people's businesses*.

When you hand your money over to a financial advisor to help you grow it, what you're really doing is providing liquidity for other entrepreneurs to grow their businesses. Meanwhile, you've deprived yourself of the ability to use that capital to invest in your own business.

For example, when you invest in Apple stock, you're helping Tim Cook grow his business. With a quarterly revenue of about $89.5 billion in the fourth quarter of 2023[5], I'm not sure he needs your help... Don't get me wrong, I love Apple. I use Apple products every day. But Apple doesn't need more of my money. My business needs more of my money. Why should I invest in Apple stock when I could invest in growing my own business?

When you invest in the financial market, you're no longer betting on yourself. You're betting on someone else. You're

---

[5]   "Apple reports fourth quarter results." Apple, November 2, 2023. Press release.

relinquishing control of your capital to your financial advisor, who is going to use it to help you bet on another entrepreneur.

You got where you are today by betting on yourself. Are you really going to change your winning formula?

And the reward for handing over your dollars to another entrepreneur isn't even spectacular. Are you really going to let go of control over your capital just so you can get, on average, a mere 8% return in the marketplace? (which is an illusion and that's before taxes eat away at it…) Simply put, it's not worth it.

When your capital is tied up in investments, you begin to have liquidity issues. When you need capital to hire a key employee, invest in new software, or capture a one-in-a-million opportunity such as acquiring a competitor, you may find that you don't have the liquidity available to do so… Because your capital is busy helping other business owners grow their businesses.

Black Swans & Gray Rhinos

Tying up your liquidity in investments can be dangerous…

What happens if there's a black swan event, which is an event that no one sees coming, or a gray rhino event, which is an event that everyone can see, hear, and feel coming…

If your liquidity is tied up in the market, what position will you be in as a business owner? Will you have access to emergency funds?

At the time of writing this book, the COVID-19 pandemic, which was a total black swan event, is just four years behind us. We can all remember what it was like when the whole world shut down… Before PPP loans were introduced, many business owners had no idea how they were going to stay afloat. Yet those businesses who had liquidity available were less anxious than those who had all of their liquidity tied up in the markets.

What would your business look like if we experienced another black swan event? Would you be in a better situation than you were in March of 2020 or a worse situation?

When you have no liquidity but need capital, whether you're dealing with a black swan event or simply capturing an opportunity, you've put yourself in a position where you'll need to go to a bank, get approved for a loan, and take on debt.

> *"The only people that a bank will loan money to are the very people who don't need it."*
>
> –Mark Twain

The challenge with banks is that they will lend you money when you don't need it, and they won't lend you money when you desperately need it. There's not a human being on the planet that can't relate to that, unless your last name is Buffett or Bezos.

Weathering the Seasons

What about planning for the seasons of a business? No business has consistent revenue across the 12 months of a year. You have a summer, when your revenue is at its height because demand for your product or service is highest, a spring, when you're planning campaigns and building momentum, a fall, when your revenue begins to taper off, and a winter, when your revenue is at its lowest... And when, if you don't have liquidity, you could have major cashflow issues.

Not only are you struggling to fund new endeavors such as expanding your team or leveling up your software, but you're now struggling to make payroll and pay the bills. This happens even with successful business owners... They have more than enough capital to afford all of these things, but because this capital is tied up in investments, it's as if they don't have it at all.

A Cashflow Crisis

Most businesses deliver a product or service before they get paid. For example, a doctor performs surgery on a patient and then collects the bill after the fact. Sometimes, there is a months-long delay between the product or service being delivered and the payment.

This means you've already had to pay the expenses associated with selling your product or service, whether it's employees' salaries, manufacturing expenses, or paying for electricity in the office. You had to pay these expenses upfront to be able to deliver your product or service. Money leaks out of your business...

In a perfect world, your clients would pay you at the same time as you paid these expenses. In case you haven't noticed, we don't live in a perfect world.

What happens if you have a slow month and it becomes difficult to collect on accounts receivable? Meanwhile, to stay in business, you still have to pay the upfront expenses necessary to sell your product or service. This could quickly spiral into a cashflow problem... And if you don't have reserves, you would be reliant on a bank loan to stay afloat. You may have to put up assets of the business, such as equipment or the building, or even personally guarantee a loan.

This is a terrible scenario, but it could get worse. You could go out of business because you don't have cashflow, which is the lifeline of the business. And if you're on the hook for a bank loan but have no income from the business coming in, the bank can take all the assets of the business and sell it. Worse, you could go bankrupt and the bank could come after your personal assets.

Is there a way to position or warehouse your excess capital without tying up your liquidity and putting yourself at risk of a cashflow crisis?

"I'll Just Sell!"

Many business owners would read the above and think, "If I need money, I'll just sell more products or services." Okay… But you sell physical products. What are your payment terms with your vendors? Do you even have the money to buy more products from your vendors so you can sell them? It's the same with services… Do you have the money to cover the overhead expenses of selling more services? Could you even afford to hire another employee to fulfill your services? And how are you going to get more sales? Can you afford to hire another salesperson?

In a real liquidity crunch and a challenging economy, many business owners think that they would just sell the business.

But do you know the value of the business now? Do you know the value when you are going to sell it? How did you determine the value? Do you have a buyer lined up?

Reality check… If you have to sell the business to generate capital, your business is probably not worth millions of dollars. Who would want to buy a business that has cashflow management problems?

If you don't know how much your business is worth (from an appraisal, not from a guess) and you don't have a buyer lined up, you can't rely on selling to be a viable option.

Without having a strategy around generating more sales or selling your business, these plans are just based on hope.

Questions For Clarity

Beyond the challenge of finding a vehicle to position or warehouse your excess capital, now that your business is successful and consistently produces excess revenue, you may be starting to consider your bigger financial picture…

As you do this, it's important that you ask the right questions.

The quality of the questions we ask ourselves determines the quality of our lives.

Your thinking determines your actions, which determine what your life looks like. If you want to change your life, you need to change your thinking. You do that by asking yourself better questions.

It's time for you to think about your life and business in a different way. Here are some questions for you to think about.

Family:

1. If both spouses are working in the business, what happens if one or both spouses die and/or become disabled or incapacitated and cannot work anymore?
2. How will this impact the family's income and lifestyle?
3. What happens to the family if the spouse who is the breadwinner dies and/or becomes disabled or incapacitated and cannot work anymore?
4. How will this impact the family's income and lifestyle?

5. What happens if the spouse who is the homemaker and managing the household and taking care of the children dies and/or becomes disabled or incapacitated and cannot manage the household and take care of the children?

Do you have a family strategy and contingency plan?

Business:

1. What happens to your business if you and/or your partner(s) die or become disabled and/or incapacitated?
2. In the event of a partner's death, will you and the other remaining partners be buying out the spouse and family of the deceased partner?
3. How will you come up with the capital to do that?
4. Who runs the business? Is there a documented succession and/or contingency plan currently?
5. Do you have a buy/sell agreement in place for the partners? How will this be funded if needed?

Do you have a business strategy and contingency plan?

Financial Health:

1. Do you know what return you will have to earn on your capital to live in the future like you live today adjusted for inflation?
2. Do you know how much capital you should be saving each month or annually set aside for the future to live like you live today adjusted for inflation?

3. Do you know how long you will have to work in your business at the same pace to put enough money aside to last your life?
4. Do you know how much you will have to reduce your standard of living if you don't do something different?
5. Do you have a financial strategy that works regardless of whether the markets, taxes, or inflation go up, go down, or stay the same?

Download A Free Report That Shares How Business Owners & Their Families Can Achieve Certainty, Predictability & Clarity:

https://producerswealth.com/polaris

As you move toward your financial future, you need a vehicle that solves these challenges and allows you to continue to bet on yourself. Believe it or not, that perfect vehicle is out there…

CHAPTER 2

The Perfect Vehicle

Let me tell you a story about my first mentor. He was an older guy I met at a real estate investment club in 2001. He explained to me that in the 1970s, he would take $100,000, go to the bank, and put that $100,000 in a certificate of deposit. This might sound insane today, but in the 70s, the returns were 10% or higher.

After he did that, he would go to the exact same bank and say, "Mr. Banker, I have a CD in your bank for $100,000. Can I get a loan that is secured by that $100,000?"

The banker would say, "Of course." My mentor would get a loan for $90,000 at 9%. He would then go and buy real estate with that $90,000. After buying the real estate, he would then pay the loan down with the income he was generating from the real estate. All the while, he had $100,000 compounding in the bank at a rate of 10%. His original $100,000 was growing, while he borrowed against it to create an asset that generated revenue, had great tax benefits, and appreciated in value through proper management. He would repeat this strategy over and over again... When he told me this story, my mind was blown.

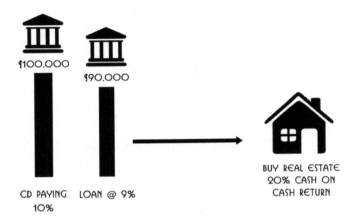

This is a powerful strategy. But what is ten times more powerful than that is doing that exact same strategy with a dividend-paying whole life insurance policy with a mutual insurance company. When you fund your life insurance policy and build up cash value, your cash value grows tax-free, while the CD wouldn't. You can establish a line of credit against the cash value of up to 90-95%. Then, you can take that money and invest in your business.

Your money is growing uninterrupted, compounding tax-free in your policy. You took a policy loan secured by it to finance the growth of your business. You, as the business owner, the #1 asset of the business, are protected because there is also a death benefit on the policy, as well as a disability rider, meaning that if you become disabled, that policy is paid up and you don't lose the policy or the cash value. Eventually, you can take money from the policy to fund the back end of your life tax-free as a business owner.

Essentially, life insurance is the perfect vehicle that allows you to adopt my mentor's strategy and add rocket fuel to it.

It's Time to Come Clean... This Book Is About Life Insurance

When you read the words "life insurance" at the end of that story, did you flinch? Did you imagine a slimy salesperson peddling a scam? Did you contemplate throwing the book across the room and running away?

Yes, it's true, this is a book about a life insurance strategy that is part of a holistic wealth strategy.

Specifically, this is a book about using a whole life insurance policy with a mutual insurance company to store your excess capital and become your own bank.

Life insurance doesn't quite have a glowing reputation... At a cocktail party, if someone asks "What do you do?" and the person says they're a lawyer, doctor, or nuclear physicist, everyone will say "Oh, wow." They'll smile, nod, and ask follow-up questions like, "So what type of law do you practice? Where did you go to medical school? Do you build rockets?" But if the person answers "What do you do?" with "I sell life insurance," not only will there not be a follow-up question, but everyone will leave the person's presence immediately.

If life insurance is so widely hated, why bother talking about it?

Before you throw the book across the room and swear off life insurance forever, consider this: what if this solution could provide you with...

1. Clarity (which turns into Confidence)
2. Certainty
3. Predictability
4. A Tax-Free Alternative
5. Family Contingency Planning
6. Business Contingency Planning
7. Asset Protection (For your #1 asset... you)

If a solution could provide you with all of these things, isn't it at least worth investigating?

A whole life insurance policy with a mutual insurance company is the perfect vehicle to store your excess capital so you can maximize your control over your destiny and continue to bet on yourself.

You may have heard of this solution under other names: "infinite banking," "bank of yourself," "cashflow banking," "private reserve strategy," and more. In this book, we're going to demystify what this life insurance strategy actually means— and why many successful business owners have been using it since the mid 1800s.

The Perfect Savings Vehicle

Why is life insurance the perfect savings vehicle?

- It's safe. Your principal is guaranteed never to go down in value.
- Your capital is contractually guaranteed to grow. There's a big difference between contractual wealth and statement wealth... Contractual wealth is a private contract between you and a mutual life insurance company. By contract, your net worth increases with each and every contribution that you make. Meanwhile, a statement just gives you a snapshot of how your investments are performing. In our perfect savings vehicle, we want a contract that guarantees our wealth will grow.
- Although dividends are not guaranteed, you get to participate in the profits of the mutual life insurance carrier by receiving a dividend. They have paid dividends for over 170 years consecutively.
- The tax advantages are fantastic. Tax-free growth, dividends are tax-free, tax-free access to savings, tax-free distributions for retirement, and a tax-free death benefit.
- The death benefit of the life insurance policy is a multiple of the cash value account value, which is distributed to beneficiaries tax-free.
- There is a guaranteed death benefit so that when you pass away, your family gets capital tax-free. We don't want a 401k or traditional IRA... If you have $1 million in either of these vehicles, you can't guarantee

that your family will receive $1 million upon your death because it's tied to the equity market and is taxable. Since we can't predict what tax rates will be in the future, we can't predict how much your family will receive.

- It's not exposed to market volatility because it's not correlated to the equity markets. If the stock market goes down 50%, nothing will happen to the capital inside this vehicle.

- It gives you liquidity. You have guaranteed access to your savings for emergencies and opportunities.

- It's protected from creditors. As a business owner in the United States, you do not have to do anything wrong to be sued. You have a target on your back, and you may not even be aware of it. If you're in a situation such as a car accident, and someone finds out you're a business owner with a high net worth, they see dollar signs...

- There's a hedge against inflation. Inflation reduces the value of your capital over time. The Federal Reserve openly states that it's trying to keep inflation at 2%. [6] To beat inflation, we want a vehicle that compounds at a higher rate than inflation.

- You have full control with no strings attached. Qualified plans have more strings attached than Pinocchio had before he became a real boy... We want to find a vehicle that avoids this.

- If you become disabled, there are benefits to help you, and you will not lose the vehicle.

---

6   "Why does the Federal Reserve aim for inflation of 2 percent over the longer run?" *Board of Governors of the Federal Reserve System.* August 27, 2020.

- This vehicle is transferable so you can change the ownership and beneficiaries when and if needed.
- This vehicle is a private contract, which is very important. Why? If you have a lot of money in the bank, everybody knows. That information has been sold to third parties. But when you have a vehicle with a private contract, nobody knows you have that money unless you declare it and put it in a financial statement, and nobody knows if you access any of the cash value through a policy. There are no credit reporting agencies that your assets are reported to.
- There is flexibility of premium payments and policy loan repayments.
- You have leverage. You can place your capital as collateral for loans, allowing your capital to work in two places simultaneously.
- There are no contribution limits as there are with qualified plans like 401Ks, IRAs, and Roth IRAs.
- A track record of over 170 years as a vehicle that provides certainty, security, and predictability.

The only negative with this perfect vehicle is that you can't deduct your premiums from taxes today. (But this is okay... I'll explain why later).

The Aligned Capital Strategy™ has all of the features listed above... But wait, there's more.

You can have your cake and eat it too. You can put money in the policy and then use it in your business. This isn't just a bucket you're drawing from. You're not actually touching the cash value that continues to grow uncompounded, tax-free. You have the ability to use the money to grow your business while that money compounds and grows tax-free for you.

You might read this and think, "That sounds too good to be true." I get it. It does. But let's look at why this is possible...

On one side of the table, you put capital into your vehicle and you get all of these incredible benefits we talked about. But on the other side of the table, the life insurance company collects the premiums upfront. Just through underwriting, they're already profitable. Then, they invest that capital. When you take a policy loan, the life insurance company has two pieces of collateral, so they're protected twice. They have your death benefit and cash value, so they can guarantee you a policy loan. If you try to cash out your policy with a loan, they'll just deduct the loan from the cash value. If you pass away with an outstanding loan, the insurance carrier will deduct the loan from your death benefit.

It's a win-win situation for both you and the life insurance companies.

CHAPTER 3

Cutting Through The Noise

Why do so many people want to run away when they hear the words "life insurance"?

The problem isn't life insurance: the problem is the rampant misinformation about life insurance spread by the media and financial influencers.

The business model of the media industry is to drive as many eyeballs to their content as possible so they can run you advertisements from their sponsors. The more attention the content gets, the more advertising money it makes. We're no longer living in an Information Age–we're living in an Attention Age.

Because of the way the media makes money, you're constantly overloaded with information that you can't trust. It was designed to capture your attention, not to inform you. Many times, it doesn't matter to the creators if the information is accurate as long as it draws attention.

The media will never challenge this information because their clients are the advertisers. You may think that you, the viewer, are the media's client, but that's not the case. You're just the product being sold to hungry advertisers.

And who are the biggest ad spenders besides pharmaceutical companies and military contractors? The financial services industry. This means that the information you get from the media about financial planning and wealth management is the information the people paying the media companies want you to get. It's all marketing…

Think about how pharmaceutical ads work. At the end of the commercial, they'll say, "Ask your doctor if it's right for you." They've just pitched you a product without knowing anything about you, your medical history, or if you're even struggling with the health issue the drug is trying to solve. It's the same with financial services… Financial ads recommend you a product without knowing anything about you. Wall Street pitches you a specific mutual fund or ETF without knowing anything about your circumstances and needs.

The focus is on the product, not on you. These advertisers don't care how you use the product, how it fits into your financial strategy, or what result it will have for you, as long as you buy it. Once they have your money, they send you off with a, "Well, hope that works out okay for you."

Beyond advertising, you'll hear wildly different information on life insurance from social media and financial influencers.

You might see TikTok and YouTube gurus presenting life insurance as an exotic solution… though it's been around for over 170 years. These influencers paint a picture of all of the amazing benefits of life insurance without actually understanding it. They promise the world, portraying life insurance as a "get-rich-quick hack." They combine it with dubious strategies like buying cars to get rich or using exotic trust and foundation strategies to "never pay taxes again."

Meanwhile, other influencers are naysayers. Dave Ramsey says that life insurance is the worst place to put your money and that it's only good for the agents that sell you the life insurance. Suze Orman says that you should never buy permanent life insurance under any circumstance. Many other financial celebrities say that you should buy term insurance and invest the rest in a diversified portfolio of stocks, bonds, and mutual funds.

Whether you're listening to the pro-life-insurance crowd or the anti-life-insurance crowd, you need a shower when you're done.

No matter who you listen to, everyone has an agenda to promote or a product to sell. And with trust in institutions at an all-time low, many people are left wondering whose voice to listen to.

How Strong is Your Opinion?

If you ask 100 people how they feel about Pit Bulls, you'll probably hear everyone answer 1 of 3 ways. Some people are totally for Pit Bulls, others are totally opposed to Pit Bulls, and others can see both sides.

But if you ask 100 people how they feel about life insurance, you'll get 100 different answers. And not just different answers... Extremely emotional, passionate answers.

Everybody hates insurance. It's impossible not to hate insurance because most people have insurance that they have to pay every single month, every single quarter, every single year, without ever reaping the benefits of that insurance.

And if they do get to use the benefits, as with, for example, homeowner's insurance, their insurance costs go up immediately after filing their claim.

It's no wonder most people have a bad impression of life insurance...

The life insurance product that gets sold the most often is term insurance. 99% of term policies don't pay out...[7] Term life insurance is basically a bet with the insurance company on whether you will die in a certain time frame or not. For the 10, 20, or 30 years that you pay premiums, if you die, your beneficiaries get the death benefit tax-free. But if you don't die, the insurance company gets to keep all of the premiums in that time frame. It's a bet that you hope you lose, because if you win, you're 6 feet under the ground, but losing the bet means you've wasted money.

---

[7] Penn State University study, 1993

My goal with this book is to get you to forget what you think you know about life insurance, understand this strategy, and determine if it is right for you with a full understanding of how it works. The mission of my company is to elevate the financial well-being of business owners and their families. Life insurance, if leveraged properly, has the potential to do this.

Let go of all the misinformation about life insurance that other people have put into your head... It's time to arm ourselves with facts.

If something you thought to be true wasn't true, when would you want to know about it?

"Your assumptions are windows on the world. Scrub them off every once in a while, or the light won't come in."

--Isaac Asimov

It's Tried and True!

From the way that some misinformed influencers talk, you'd think that life insurance was an exotic solution that just fell out of the sky...

But this strategy is over 170 years old and has been used by banks, financial institutions, corporations, and the wealthiest families and individuals in the United States for all of that history.

Farmers have used life insurance as a cashflow management system for over 170 years. Farmers deal with the "seasons" of a business in a much more literal and direct way than the rest of us. They need to plan to have capital available even when it's winter and they aren't able to grow any crops. They may not be making a profit every season, but they still need capital available to hire employees, plant the seeds, work the land, pay for fertilizer, and nurture the crops until the season when they're finally ready to be harvested. Then, when the farmer takes the crops to market, there is a massive windfall.

Like the farmer, every business has seasons… Your sales may peak in Q2 and lull in Q4, but you need to have cash on hand each month to pay your employees, develop marketing campaigns, test new products, and do anything else that is necessary to keep the business running. Why not leverage the tried and tested strategy that farmers have used to combat this issue since long before your grandparents were born?

Most people see 401ks as a "safer" savings strategy, but life insurance is over 130 years older than 401ks… Life insurance was the primary savings vehicle for Americans until 401ks were launched in the 1980s.

Not only have Mutual Life Insurance Companies been around for over 170 years in their current format—they have been profitable every single year for over 170 years consecutively. There is a carrier that has been around since 1847 and has paid dividends every single year consecutively since then. Think about all of the turbulent historical events we've had since 1850… We've had the American Civil War, two World

Wars, the Great Depression, economic crashes... The world's monetary system changed several times throughout that time period, and these companies were profitable every year.

Mutual Life Insurance companies have been through almost every single economic scenario imaginable over the last 170 years and still delivered on their promises.

What are the safeguards of mutual life insurance companies?

There are six layers of protection for policyholders of dividend-paying whole life insurance with mutual life insurance carriers...

1. All life insurance companies in the U.S., including mutual companies, are regulated by state insurance departments. Regulations ensure that these companies maintain certain solvency standards, keep adequate reserves to pay future claims, and follow fair practices in dealing with consumers.
2. If a life insurance carrier finds itself in financial difficulty, the state commissioner's office can take control of the carrier and run the carrier on behalf of the shareholders.
3. In the event that a life insurance company fails, state life insurance guaranty associations provide a safety net for policyholders. Coverage limits vary by state, but these associations work to protect policyholders by guaranteeing continued coverage or refunding a portion of policy values.

4. Life insurance carriers are audited regularly by independent rating companies. You want your policy with the top-rated financial mutual lie insurance carriers that have a track record of paying dividends for over 170 years.

5. If an insurance company declares bankruptcy, regulators will usually seek another insurance company to assume the policies of the insolvent insurer. This process involves transferring the policies and associated liabilities to a financially stable company, ensuring continued coverage for policyholders.

6. The Federal government can step in and bail out a life insurance carrier. In 2008, AIG, a company that is a stock company and not a mutual life insurance carrier, was bailed out by the Federal government.

Mutual life insurance carriers are owned by the policyholders, who are the shareholders, so interests are aligned. When mutual life insurance carriers run their business in the best interest of their policyholders, more people want to buy policies with them.

Meanwhile, stock life insurance carriers are owned by the owners of the stock of the company. The business is run in the best interest of the stockholders so that more institutions would want to buy their stock. Vanguard and Blackrock are the biggest holders of AIG stock currently[8].

How many publicly listed companies on the New York Stock Exchange or on the equity markets do you know that have

---

[8]   *Yahoo Finance.* March 13, 2024.

been in existence for 100+ years and have been profitable every single year consecutively for over 100 years?

During these 170 years, many wealthy, influential people have used life insurance to achieve incredible things...

When Walt Disney wanted to launch Disneyland, no bank would lend him money for what seemed like a crazy idea... So he leveraged the cash value of his life insurance policy to build his dream[9]. Now, the entertainment empire he built is worth billions, and Disney is recognized as a visionary whose theme parks are beloved, iconic fixtures of American culture.

Ray Kroc, the CEO who turned McDonald's into the most successful fast-food corporation in the world, relied heavily on the cash value of his life insurance to get the franchise off the ground. For the first eight years he was CEO, he didn't take a salary and used his two cash-value life insurance policies to overcome constant cashflow problems. He used the policies to cover the salaries of key employees and pay for unforeseen expenses. He even used some of the money to create an advertising campaign around the infamous Ronald McDonald, which boosted the franchise's popularity[10].

Pampered Chef founder Doris Christopher funded her first inventory using a policy loan from her cash value life insurance.

---

[9]   Beattie, Andrew. "Walt Disney: How Entertainment Became an Empire." *Investopedia*. November 27, 2022.

[10]   Anderson, Brian. "6 famous brands started or saved by life insurance." *Think Advisor*. April 6, 2012.

Now, the company has grown into a multimillion-dollar business known internationally[11].

U.S. presidents like John F. Kennedy, Howard Taft, William McKinley, and Franklin D. Roosevelt have utilized dividend-paying whole life insurance policies. Current president Joe Biden has six dividend-paying whole life insurance policies with a mutual life insurance carrier[12].

Think Like A Rockefeller...

At one point in history, the Rockefellers and the Vanderbilts were two of the wealthiest families in the United States. Today, the Rockefeller family has not only protected their wealth but grown it significantly with each generation. Meanwhile, the Vanderbilt family still has universities and buildings named after them... But at a recent family reunion, they didn't have any millionaires in attendance, except for Anderson Cooper, but his millions came from CNN, not the family fortune. The Vanderbilts squandered their wealth, while the Rockefellers protected and increased it with each generation.

While the Vanderbilts divided their wealth among the family with no strategy, the Rockefellers kept the capital together in a family bank using life insurance contracts[13]. You don't have to be a Rockefeller to do what the Rockefellers do.

---

[11]   Anderson, Brian. "6 famous brands started or saved by life insurance." *Think Advisor*. April 6, 2012.

[12]   Bell, Alison. "Joe Biden Owns a Security Benefit Variable Annuity." *Think Advisor*. October 6, 2020.

[13]   "Rockefellers v. Vanderbilts: How It Started & How It's Going." *Trust & Will*.

The family office model in the US is based on the way the Rockefellers managed their wealth. Family Offices are wealth management firms that manage an ultra-high-net-worth family's wealth. With a Family Office, wealthy families have access to multiple advisors under one roof, all of whom collaborate to align the family's financial strategies. Family Offices buy as much life insurance for the families whose wealth they manage as life insurance carriers will sell the family. Like the Rockefellers, the wealthy families of today (and the experts who manage their money within the Family Office), understand that life insurance is a tried, true, unbeatable strategy for preserving wealth for generations to come.

How Banks, Corporations, and Universities Win With Life Insurance

Throughout society, many organizations and institutions use life insurance to accomplish their goals. The next time you hear an influencer portraying life insurance as a crackpot strategy, consider all of the commonplace ways life insurance is used every day...

Banks

Tier one capital is the safest capital that a bank has. Due to banking regulations, banks have to have a certain amount of capital in tier one. The majority of tier-one capital is placed in life insurance contracts because of the guaranteed tax-free growth and death benefits.

> *"Banks, when it comes to investing their own money, don't follow the conventional wisdom of putting their cash into mutual funds, stocks, hedge funds, term life insurance or risky real estate deals. Instead, they place a large portion of their vital reserves into high cash value life insurance or whole life insurance policies."*
>
> --Barry James Dyke

Banks buy as much life insurance as part of their Tier 1 capital as they are legally allowed to. According to the FDIC, banks are the largest purchasers of life insurance in the United States.

Corporations

Large corporations use life insurance as an incentive for CEO packages. If the CEO stays for a certain time period, such as ten years, they walk away with tax-free money in their life insurance policies. The longer the CEO stays, the longer the money grows, so CEOs who devote decades of service to the company are rewarded with millions of dollars of tax-free capital in a life insurance policy. Corporations also use key person insurance to hire and retain employees and protect themselves when they lose key employees. For example, GE has helped its CEO Jeffrey Immelt amass $22 million in life insurance coverage[14]. Kenneth Lay, former CEO of Enron, had a life insurance policy funded by the company, which meant that his assets were protected even when he was found

---

[14]   Melin, Anders. "GE's death perk for Immelt: A $22 million life insurance benefit." *Think Advisor.* August 20, 2015.

guilty of fraud[15]. I don't recommend committing fraud, but this case goes to show how effective life insurance is for asset protection. If it can protect the assets of a criminal involved in a major scandal, it can protect you from creditors in a run-of-the-mill business lawsuit.

Universities

Stanford University was founded with life insurance. After Leland and Jane Stanford lost their son to typhoid fever, they focused their efforts and wealth on helping other people's children and launched Stanford University. In 1891, the first 555 students enrolled at Stanford University. But after Leleand died in 1893, the university struggled financially. Not wanting to give up on her late husband's dream, Jane used Leland's life insurance policy proceeds to fund operations and pay faculty, allowing Stanford University to weather a dangerous period of financial distress and grow into the success it is today[16].

College sports teams often use life insurance as an incentive to attract top coaching talent and build the reputations of their sports programs. College football coach Jim Harbaugh, who led Michigan to a national championship in 2023, had a compensation package structured with a $2 million annual life insurance premium[17].

---

[15]   *Split Dollar Life Insurance Agreement – Enron Corp. and the Kenneth L. Lay (KLL) & Linda Phillips Lay (LPL) Family Partnership Ltd.* April 22, 1994.

[16]   Anderson, Brian. "6 famous brands started or saved by life insurance." *Think Advisor.* April 6, 2012.

[17]   "Harbaugh up to $7M with Michigan paying insurance premiums." *Associated Press.* August 18, 2016.

And You!

The best part of this 170-year-old solution that has been leveraged by banks, corporations, universities, presidents, and the wealthiest people in America? You have access to this same solution... You don't have to be Walt Disney, a Rockefeller, the President of the United States, or the founder of an Ivy League university to use this strategy to Get Wealthy For Sure™.

CHAPTER 4

Aligned Capital Strategy™

Let me introduce you to the Aligned Capital Strategy™.

The Aligned Capital Strategy™ uses a dividend-paying whole life insurance policy with a mutual life insurance company, structured with a high cash value and a low death benefit, as a savings vehicle that you can use to effectively become your own bank and Get Wealthy For Sure™.

I built it because I couldn't find any other solution that worked...

When I set up my first life insurance policy, I discovered it was set up wrong. I went to another financial professional, who fixed the policy. When it was set up correctly, I told him, "Great, now how do I use this to create my own infinite banking system?"

His response was, "I don't know. I don't have one of these policies myself."

I said, "What do you mean you don't have one of these policies yourself? You're selling something that you don't have?"

I then decided to become as educated as possible on this strategy. I read as many books on cashflow management as I could... I talked to people in my network about how they used this system in a family office... When people I knew were interested in setting up this strategy, I would refer them to the second financial professional I went to, but guess what happened?

They would come to me and say, "I don't know how to use this, and neither does my financial professional. Can you share how you use it?" I began to coach people on how to use this strategy. I saw there was a massive opportunity to merge the financial services world with the business owner world and help people implement this strategy. Thus, the Aligned Capital Strategy™ was born...

I've been personally using this strategy for a decade and a half, and now, my family has 11 policies in our banking system.

Even if you think you get this strategy, could you implement it correctly 11 times? I don't say this to be arrogant but to challenge you to lean on the knowledge of those who have already used this strategy rather than trying to learn from experience (and potentially lose time and money in the process).

The Aligned Capital Strategy™ gave me the power to bet on myself...

My family and I have used this strategy to pay off my wife's student loans, start my firm, invest in supportive businesses, and invest in real estate.

Let me tell you a fun story... Imagine you're sitting around with friends, drinking wine at a winery that you co-own, relaxing while your kids run around outside–and all of this was made possible because of life insurance.

This isn't just a daydream... I've used a life insurance policy loan to invest in a historic winery that happens to be the third-oldest winery in the United States. A handful of my clients have heard about this and invested in this same winery using policy loans from the life insurance policies I helped them set up.

There's not a lot of financial vehicles you can do that with!

The Road Ahead

In the rest of the book, we'll explore the pillars of the Aligned Capital Strategy™:

Chapter 5: What the Aligned Capital Strategy Isn't™: What is the difference between this strategy and term life insurance? If you already have the wrong kind of life insurance policy in place, is there anything you can do? In this chapter, I'll introduce you to the Universal Life Rescue™ and the Policy Clean Up Strategy™.

Chapter 6: Get Wealthy for Sure™: The Aligned Capital Strategy™ is not a Get Rich Quick strategy. We're going to Get Wealthy For Sure™. Before implementing the strategy, we're going to take the time to understand the problem we face, the strategy that solves the problem, and why this strategy is superior to other options.

Chapter 7: Human Capital and Relationship Capital: For this strategy to work, you need to build an aligned team of financial professionals. In this chapter, we'll break down what to look for in a life insurance advisor–and reveal why your family is the most important part of your team.

Chapter 8: Capital Creation and Financial Capital: When you want to create more financial capital, focus on increasing your intellectual capital and relationship capital. Once this strategy is in place, increase its impact by growing your business and funneling more capital into your banking system.

Chapter 9: Capital Capture: We're going to plug all of your cashflow leaks by modeling our system after the way banks capture capital.

Chapter 10: Cashflow Creation → Capital Growth: Now that you have your banking system set up, you can use it to finance the growth of your business and invest in other assets.

Chapter 11: Capital Control, Tax, Asset, and Estate Planning: In this chapter, we'll introduce a tax strategy that helps you retain more of your capital. We'll also cover asset protection and estate planning strategies that work in conjunction with your banking system.

By the end of the book, you'll have a clear understanding of how the Aligned Capital Strategy™ works so you can decide if this vehicle is the key to your financial future.

CHAPTER 5

What the Aligned Capital Strategy™ Isn't

First, let's break down what the Aligned Capital Strategy™ isn't. It isn't an IUL, a Variable Universal Life Policy, a Whole Life Insurance policy tied to a market index, Term Insurance, or any other exotic insurance vehicle.

We're using the tried-and-tested, battle-hardened, dividend-paying whole life insurance policy with a mutual life insurance company that's been around since the mid-1800s.

Should I Buy Term Insurance?

People often ask me, "Should I buy term insurance or whole life insurance?" You should probably have both!

Stop thinking in terms of product and start thinking in terms of strategy. With this banking strategy, we're trying to maximize cash value and give you a warehouse to store your capital. A properly structured whole life policy allows you to maximize cash value and minimize the death benefit.

Meanwhile, term insurance solves a different problem. It provides a death benefit that protects your future potential income for your family in case of your death.

For example, if you make $1 million dollars a year and die unexpectedly in your 40s, that's a $20 million loss to your family. If you have kids, this financial loss could impact their education opportunities and put a strain on your grieving spouse to make an income to make up for this loss.

If you buy convertible term insurance, you can protect this potential income for your family. With a convertible term policy, you can convert the policy to more dividend-paying whole life policies without medical underwriting, so it protects your ability to keep adding dividend-paying whole life insurance policies even if something happens to you health-wise. You lock in your health today. For example, if you receive a cancer diagnosis or develop cardiac problems as you age, you may find it impossible to be insured. A convertible term policy prevents you from facing this issue.

There is a purpose to both term and whole life. Having both protects you and gives you more options as your net worth grows.

Start thinking about strategy and not just products!

Universal Life Rescue

"You've got to know when to hold 'em, know when to fold 'em, know when to walk away, know when to run."

--Kenny Rogers

Universal life insurance is classified as permanent life insurance, but it is completely different from whole life insurance. The most well-known universal life policies are indexed universal life (IUL) and variable universal life (VUL).

Universal Life uses a renewable term with a bucket that is tied to something, depending on if it is an IUL or VUL. IULs are tied to a specific stock index, like the S&P 500, while VULs are tied to a specific stock portfolio that you can manage.

Dividend-paying whole life insurance policies with mutual life insurance carriers have been around since the mid-1800s, but universal life insurance was only created in the 1980s as a response to 401ks.

Before 401ks were invented, the average American never invested in the stock market–it was reserved for affluent individuals such as doctors, lawyers, and business owners. But when 401ks were rolled out, all of a sudden, the majority of the American working population changed from defined benefit plans to defined contribution plans and invested in the stock market. The stock market skyrocketed…

People no longer wanted to buy life insurance because it was seen as boring compared to the massive spike in the stock market. Life insurance carriers ended up designing Universal Life policies, which took a chassis of renewable term insurance and added a bundle of stocks or an index to it. People could now buy life insurance and invest in stocks at the same time, which was a very sexy sell.

Yet Universal Life policies are not the perfect savings vehicle...

Universal Life is based on a renewal term that renews every year at your current age, meaning that your insurance costs increase as you get older.

Also, Universal Life policies are tied to the market, which can go up, down, and sideways. There's no guaranteed growth in this vehicle... If the market goes down, there's no growth in the policy at all for that year.

There is a cap and floor in Universal Life policies, meaning that there is an upper limit to what you can earn. You don't get the full benefit from the potential of where the stock market is going. If the stock market goes to 20% and your ceiling is 10%, you only get 10%. On the other hand, a floor places a limit on what you can lose. If the stock market is down 20%, rather than losing money, you just earn nothing that year.

But the cost of your insurance rises year by year, regardless of how the stock market is doing... Meaning you may be paying an exorbitant fee for an investment vehicle that earns you $0 that year.

In Universal Life policies like Index Universal Life and Variable Universal Life, there is a crossover point where the policy is not growing the capital in the policy but consuming it.

Essentially, buying Universal Life means you're either:

1) Predicting that the stock market will be up every year... Yeah right. This would be like if the weatherman tried to make a forecast using tarot cards.
2) Accepting that you're not going to get returns every year, even though you're paying increasingly higher costs for this life insurance.

What starts to happen as people with Universal Life policies age is that the policies that were once affordable become prohibitively expensive. These people were promised by financial professionals in the 1980s, "Don't worry about the cost of insurance rising each year. Your returns in the market will be so high that it'll offset the cost of insurance." Unfortunately, that's not reality. The promised high returns never materialized, so the client can't afford the premiums anymore and loses the policy.

The New York Department of Financial Services (NYDS) issued an alert to New Yorkers after receiving over 1400 complaints over a five-year period for universal life policies. Superintendent Linda Lacewell issued a statement:

"The Department has seen many cases of consumers who purchased universal life insurance and who made payments for years, thinking their premium payment would not change or that their coverage would remain in effect. But many found that their policies had lapsed (were no longer in effect) with little to no (cash) value due to declines in interest rates, market volatility, and other factors, or they were required to pay large additional premium payments to keep their coverage in effect.

The internal charges of universal life policies can increase every year. Ongoing premium payments, the policy's existing cash value, and ongoing interest credits (or investment performance in the case of variable universal life insurance) are all used to cover the policies and internal charges which increase each year as the insured gets older, and can be very high in later years."[18]

Pick your favorite search engine and type in "universal life lawsuits." You could spend hours in this internet rabbit hole, reading countless stories of real people who feel they were never told that these policies would one day become unaffordable.

So, if you have a Universal Life policy, what can be done?

Take a deep breath… There is a path forward.

It's called the Universal Life Rescue.

---

[18]   Festa, Elizabeth. "New York Financial Superintendent Lacewell Warns of Hidden Costs in Universal Life Policies." Think Advisor. February 22, 2019.

You might know about a 1031 exchange in real estate. In life insurance, there's a similar strategy called a 1035 exchange, where you can rescue your universal life policy when it becomes unaffordable. You can roll over the equity that's left in the Universal Life policy into a dividend-paying Whole Life policy with a mutual life insurance carrier. When you do this, you can still have a tax-free retirement and a tax-free death benefit to leave a legacy to your beneficiaries–all with a locked-in insurance cost that will not rise over time. You'll be able to pull from your new policy for a tax-free retirement without the burden of skyrocketing insurance costs that eat up the cash value of the policy.

Policy Clean Up Strategy™

Some people understand the difference between Universal Life and Whole Life. They go to a retail insurance professional or their financial advisor, completely informed on this strategy... Yet they end up with a policy structured completely wrong.

For the Aligned Capital Strategy™ to work, we want the lowest possible death benefit and the highest possible cash value. Yet an advisor or insurance salesperson who doesn't understand this strategy might give you a $10 million death benefit with no cash value... If this happens, you've just bought a very expensive whole life insurance policy.

Not every life insurance professional is created equal. It's important to find someone who focuses on life insurance as a savings vehicle, not on life insurance for the death benefit.

Asking your stockbroker to set up your life insurance policy would be like asking your dentist to do brain surgery. This is a specialized policy that not every financial professional has knowledge of.

If you end up with a policy with a high death benefit and low cash value, you might look at your policy and find you have zero cash value in year one. If this policy is set up correctly, you should have a significant portion of your premium already available in cash value from the moment you fund the policy. If you look at your policy two years in (or if you look at the two-year projections) and you have zero cash value, if you've been making your premium payments, something's wrong. Your policy is not structured correctly.

A stock insurance company is not like a mutual insurance company. A stock insurance company is managed on behalf of the stockholders, so they have an incentive to attract people to buy their stock on the New York Stock Exchange and make risky investments.

Meanwhile, a mutual life insurance company manages the company in the best interest of its policyholders. If they do that, they'll be able to make consistent dividend payouts, which attracts other people to buy their policies.

Would you rather buy a life insurance policy from a company that is incentivized to prioritize you or one that is incentivized to prioritize stockholders and leave you as an afterthought?

If you have a policy that has been set up incorrectly, we can rescue your policy by performing a 1035 exchange, moving the capital in your policy to a new policy that's structured correctly and has cash value available for use immediately.

Even if you think you have something set up incorrectly, it's not the end of the world. We can help "rescue" your policy and give you a second chance to succeed with this strategy.

But even if you've done everything correctly, it can still go wrong...

Imagine you went to the right company, went to an agent who knew what he was doing, set up the right vehicle, knew that it was structured correctly, and used it how you were supposed to use it. Then what happens? The life insurance carrier changes its organizational structure and goes from a mutual life insurance carrier to a stock insurance carrier.

This isn't just a horror story... At the time this book was written, it just happened with Ohio National[19].

If this happens to you, or if you were one of the unlucky people affected by Ohio National's demutualization, it isn't the end of the road. We can help you roll that policy over into a mutual life insurance carrier that has no intention to ever demutualize.

---

[19]   Turner, Barbara A., President and CEO, Memo to Policyholders, Ohio National Financial Services, 2021

CHAPTER 6

Get Wealthy For Sure™

Despite what misinformed influencers may tell you, life insurance is not a hack to "get rich quick." If you find a way to "get rich quick," let me know... Unless you happen to be a lottery winner or have inherited millions from a mysterious, long-lost relative, there is no way to get rich quick.

That's okay... We can do something better. We can Get Wealthy For Sure™.

But before you implement the Aligned Capital Strategy™ to Get Wealthy For Sure™, you need to approach it with the right mindset so your expectations match reality.

In this chapter, I'm going to show you how to think like a wealthy person so you get the most out of the Aligned Capital Strategy™...

The Power of Knowledge

"The problem in America isn't so much what people don't know; the problem is what people think they know that just ain't so."

–Will Rogers

Knowledge isn't power. The correct, applied knowledge is power.

If you don't understand the problem, the solution doesn't matter. Without an understanding of the problem you face, you'll be an easy target for people trying to sell you "solutions" that won't get you the results you want.

And even if you understand the problem and the solution, you have to take your knowledge a step further and apply what you know to take the correct action.

We all are born into this world with no say over what parents, community, and environment we are born into. Usually, we adopt the worldview and mindset of the environment we're born into. As we grow up, other people come into our lives who bring us new perspectives and new knowledge, but we all begin our lives with the knowledge base of the environment we were born into. Wherever you are today, take a step back and remember the foundation that you started with.

There are 4 types of knowledge:

1. Things we know to be true
2. Things we think we know to be true
3. Things we don't know
4. Things we don't know that we don't know

The number one thing I've learned from wealthy and successful people is that they're always interested in #4. They ask themselves, "What's my blind spot? What can I learn?"

There are three ways to increase your knowledge:

1. Through the places you go
2. Through the things you read, study, and learn
3. Through the people you meet

If you want to Get Wealthy For Sure™, determine what your own blind spots are and discover ways to increase your knowledge.

Focus on Strategies, Not Products

When you play golf, if you've spent time practicing your swing, you are positioned to play the best round of golf given your skillset. But if you buy a shiny new golf club and head to the course without taking time to build your skills, you might embarrass yourself... Or even if you do have the skills, but you choose a golf club out of your bag that's completely wrong for your position, your swing won't accomplish what you want it to. You wouldn't tee off with your putter...

On the golf course, it's all about your swing, club selection, course management, limiting your errors, and recovering from errors without massive damage when they occur.

It's not about having the golf club... It's about having the best strategy.

The best players in golf have the best strategy. Just like the best players in the game of wealth have the best strategy.

A strategy must work in any environment. It must be dynamic and flexible so you can adjust to changing circumstances and changes in assumptions. You must be able to track and manage it. It must be verifiable. There must be an immediate feedback loop. It must be simple and easy to implement. Finally, it must be holistic, aligning all the assets within your personal, business, and investment economy.

It can be very easy to drift off into a sea of misinformation and drown in the sole pursuit of a magic product."
--Donald L. Blanton

Your strategy matters, not your product. A fancy product with no strategy, or one that isn't right for the problem you're trying to solve, won't move you toward your goal...

Yet every single financial advertisement you see is trying to sell you a product. You don't see ads that say, "Let's match you with an advisor so we can map out the best strategy for you." You see ads that say, "Everyone needs to buy this stock."

You can't win with any one product. To accomplish your goals, you need a strategy to align all of your capital.

Sun Tzu's The Art of War describes the age-old strategy of divide and conquer. If you divide your enemy, it's easier to defeat them because they aren't working against you as an aligned, united front.

The British Empire perfected this strategy and used it to conquer the world. They divided populations into sub-groups and turned them against each other so they could conquer a geographic area without being stopped.

You know what's crazy to me? We understand this strategy when it comes to warfare, yet when it comes to finances, many people believe in diversifying assets.

Why would you knowingly divide your capital and resources to weaken your financial strategy?

There is a time on your journey when you do need to diversify, and there is a strategy to doing it successfully (it's not what you've been told and sold!). But there is a difference between diversifying intentionally using a thought-out strategy and doing what most people do, which is, "Oh, I've heard I should diversify my assets, so let's move some money over here into this stock... Hope that works out!"

Most people deworseify, not diversify.

Aligning your capital places you in the strongest position to Get Wealthy For Sure™.

It's the difference between executing a strategy with a united army working together in unison or executing the same strategy with a disorganized, divided army.

If you know a strategy works, why not align all of your capital into one "army" so you can execute this strategy with maximum effect?

Why Not Just Invest in the Stock Market?

"I suppose if I were to give advice it would be to keep out of Wall Street."

-John D. Rockefeller

Some people might read about the Aligned Capital Strategy™ and think, "I get the point, but I can get better returns in the stock market."

Sure, but the Aligned Capital Strategy™ is a savings vehicle, not an investment vehicle.

There's a massive difference between saving, investing, speculating, and gambling.

When you save, you're putting your capital into a vehicle with guarantees that it is never going to go down in value. Because of these guarantees, you get a very conservative return.

Investing is when you place capital in a vehicle, taking on a massive risk with the hopes of getting a bigger return–but you can lose some or all of the capital that you put in the vehicle.

You should only invest in what you know, and you should know that the more levels you move away from the investment, the less control you have over the outcome.

Saving is the bird in hand, and investing is the bird in the bush.

Then, we have speculation, which is a completely different approach. Speculation is when you can see imbalances and distortions in the marketplace and make predictions about what could happen. You're capitalizing on asymmetric opportunities in the marketplace, but you could lose some or all of your money.

Gambling is when, beyond the rules of the game, you have zero control over what the outcome will be. All you have is luck. You could lose some or all of your money to gambling. Even when you can count cards and win a lot, the house will always win since the game of gambling is designed that way.

A dividend-paying whole life insurance policy with a mutual insurance company is a guaranteed savings vehicle. You will not lose money, and your money is contractually guaranteed to grow. Your capital will be growing more conservatively tax-free since it's a savings vehicle, but you will have consistent growth and never lose a penny.

There is a massive difference between actual and average returns in the stock market. If you have $10,000 in stock and that stock goes up 100% in year 1, then falls 50% in year 2, in year 3, the stock goes back up 100%, and in year 4, it falls 50% again. Your average return in this example is 25%, yet your account balance is the exact same amount you started with in year 1 at the end of year 4: $10,000. You had a 25% return with $0 profit. We did not include any fees that were taken out in this example. If you include management fees, this account will be negative with a 25% return.

YEAR	MARKET	STARTING BALANCE	ENDING BALANCE
1	+100%	$10,000	$20,000
2	-50%	$20,000	$10,000
3	+100%	$10,000	$20,000
4	-50%	$20,000	$10,000
AVERAGE RATE OF RETURN: +25%			

GAIN REQUIRED TO MAKE UP FOR LOSS

What financial planners also do not tell their clients is how much your portfolio needs to generate in returns to make up for losses in the market.

If your portfolio loses 70% of its value, you need to have 233% in gains to make up for the 70% in losses.

Do you now see why it is more important to make sure you do not lose capital rather than chasing shiny objects and trying to find the next Apple stock or Bitcoin?

There's also a difference between pre-tax returns and post-tax returns. Let's pretend you're getting an 8% average return in the market. (The key word is pretend… Our kids play pretend, so why can't we?) Even if we're living in a fantasy pretend world where you get an 8% return, that's pre-tax. How much of your return will you get to keep after tax? The answer will be different depending on your financial situation, but the point is, your return will be less after tax. For example, if you have a 20% capital gains tax, your return might get bumped from 8% to 6.4%. So not only is your actual return less than the average return you were advertised but part of that actual return will get eaten by taxes.

"Just because you're following a well-marked trail doesn't mean that whoever made it knew where they were goin.'"

--Texas Bix Bender

Opportunity Cost

Don't fail to consider the opportunity cost of what you do with your money…

Business owners may think, "Well, I'm investing in my business and making money." That's great, but what they don't realize is that they've lost the opportunity to invest in the business while also having uninterrupted compounding in the policy.

Let's say your money is in a savings account earning 5%. Suddenly, you need to take that money out of the savings account to cover an emergency. Once you take the money out, it stops compounding. You lose the opportunity cost of the 5% the money could have earned if you had left it in the savings account.

You finance everything you purchase. You either pay interest by purchasing it with a loan or credit card, or you lose interest you could have earned by paying it with cash. Either way, there's a cost to any investment.

Let's take a look at three strategies of how we finance things to see how important opportunity costs are.

There are three fiancing characters out there in the economy, Rat Racers, Borrowers, and Producers.

RAT RACERS

Rat Racers save cash and then purchase things with cash savings, losing the ability to earn compound interest on their savings as they are always drawing down their savings to zero and then restarting the savings process.

BORROWERS

Borrowers do not save, they borrow money from banks and financial institutions and pay interest and principal to these banks and financial institutions. Borrowers are on the opposite end of a compound interest equation, always just trying to dig themselves out of a hole paying back the debt owed and getting back to zero.

PRODUCERS

Producers save and warehouse capital efficiently in assets that can be placed as collateral for loans at favorable rates and favorable and flexible repayment terms. This way they can generate uninterrupted compounded growth on their savings and finance the growth of their business or investment portfolio simultaneously.

With the Aligned Capital Strategy™, your money is working in two places simultaneously. It's in the policy compounding tax-free, but if you need to take money out of the policy, you take it as a loan, so there is no interruption to the compounding. You don't lose the opportunity cost of deciding whether to keep money invested in a vehicle or take it out to use it for an emergency or opportunity. You can have both.

Risk Management

We should all be our own wealth managers, and the biggest part of wealth management is risk management.

The stock that you buy for $1 that grows to $100 is a sexy story to tell at a cocktail party. But you will actually see bigger increases and more significant gains overall in your wealth by minimizing losses than by chasing massive gains.

Just ask my son, who's a huge baseball fan. It doesn't do you much good if you get a few major home runs early in the game if you can't stop your opponents from scoring. Sports teams have to play both offense and defense to win. Likewise, if you want to get wealthy, you need to focus on both increasing your wealth and minimizing losses.

There is a better return in managing risk and optimizing efficiency than in trying to pick the next big investment that will be a home run!

In sports, offense wins you games, but defense wins you championships.

The Value of Control

What is the value of control over your life to you? This answer will be different for everyone. You can control a lot of things in your life. You can control your mindset, and to a certain extent, your physical, mental, and spiritual health. You can control what happens in your home, with your marriage, with your children. You can control what happens in your business–who's on your team, what strategy you're implementing and executing, what the systems are, what the processes are. Yes, there are always external factors in every area of life at play, but you can control how you react to them. You can't control everything, but you can control how you think and act.

What is the value of control when it comes to your financial life? You can't control the market. You can't control the economy. You can't control the tax code. You can't control your country's leadership and the policies of the government.

There are so many unknown variables...

But there are things you can control when it comes to your wealth.

If there was a strategy that could place you in full control of your wealth, as the leader who is stewarding and managing your own assets, how much value would you place on that?

Stop Hoping and Start Preparing

Most strategies are just "hoping."

You hope someone will buy the business when you want to sell it... You hope the stock market doesn't crash... You hope you have liquidity on hand when an opportunity arises... You hope that markets are at an all-time high when you sell your stocks to access the money that you invested... (When you do this, you're "timing the markets," which is exactly what investors tell you not to do)...

Stop hoping and start preparing!

I believe in preparation over predictions. As human beings, we want to know what's going to happen tomorrow–but the reality is that we can never know what tomorrow will bring. We can "forecast" and "predict" all we want, but that's about as useful as shaking a Magic 8 ball or having our palm read by a psychic... Instead of trying to predict the future, prepare for it. Nobody could have predicted 2020... But the business owners who survived were the ones who had prepared for any crisis by having emergency liquidity on hand.

The Chinese word for crisis is "Wei Ji." Wei means crisis, and Ji means opportunity. They are one and the same. Every business owner should adopt this mindset. If we prepare for any potential crisis, when it occurs, we'll be able to not only survive, but capture opportunities that our competitors, who looked into a fogged-up crystal ball that told them the future would be easy, are unable to.

We can think of financial planning as climbing a mountain. You start at the bottom of the mountain, looking up at the peak that you want to reach. Then, you put in thirty or forty years of hard work backpacking up the mountain, accumulating assets, until, finally, you reach the top–the peak of your wealth. Now, you have to climb down the mountain on the other side, using the assets you've accumulated as income in retirement. (If retirement is even your end goal...

I don't believe in the word "retirement." Why would I want to be put out of use and stop contributing value to society? But that's a story for another book...)

Traditional financial planning tells you to put your money in the financial markets while you're climbing the mountain. But the financial markets can only go up, down, and sideways. You have no control over them. Furthermore, you've deferred your taxes to the future, when you have no idea how high tax rates will be. You also don't have a plan to cover fees and commissions... This means that as you're climbing the mountain, you have no idea how much capital will be set aside for retirement when you get to the top because you don't know what the markets or tax rates will be like at that time or how much you'll lose to fees and commissions. You're hoping that the markets are at an all-time high when you get to the summit... You're trying to "time" the markets, which is what every financial professional tells you not to do. If the market is at an all-time high, as you hope, you'll be able to turn your mountain of money into income to fund the back end of the mountain.

But what happens if you reach the top of the mountain and find that the market is not at an all-time high?

The danger of hoping is that there is no certainty. You can hope for something to happen as hard as you want, but that doesn't mean it will ever happen. When you hope, you have no control.

If you're planning to turn your assets into income when you get to the top of the mountain, why wouldn't you focus on a strategy while climbing up the mountain that gives you guarantees, predictability, security, fee transparency, and a tax strategy? Why wouldn't you eliminate the uncontrollable variables rather than hoping they work out for the best? Wouldn't you rather know with certainty how much capital you will have when you reach the summit? Wouldn't you rather climb up the mountain knowing you'll be able to climb down?

Understanding the Commitment

Before you implement the Aligned Capital Strategy™, you need to understand that it is a long-term commitment.

Once you set this vehicle up, you're going to pay into it for years. If you have a place where you can position capital that is growing tax-free, and you can access this capital at any given point in time, and this vehicle guarantees that your net worth will increase with every single contribution that you make, would you want to stop putting money in there, or would you want to put as much money in there as you can?

Even if you get a large sum of money or want to move money from your retirement account, this strategy is about the long-term results, not the quick wins.

And even if you start late, this commitment is for the rest of your life. You're not going to trade in and out of life insurance. We're playing the long game...

Wealthy families think three or four generations ahead. They're focused on preserving wealth for their great-grandchildren. When family offices make investments, they focus on making investments for 100 years. They don't invest in the flashy tech startups that are hot today but gone in five years. They make investments that they believe will be around for the next 100 years because their goal is to preserve wealth across generations of the family.

Meanwhile, the average person is upset if their investments don't make them rich in twelve months, or they freak out if the market is down today. Don't focus on today or even this year... Focus on the big picture.

This strategy is about consistent discipline... If we were a baseball team, we would be the team that gets base hits and has a strong defense, not the team that gets a few flashy home runs but loses the game.

Let go of any illusions that you'll be able to use this strategy to get rich overnight and win one game. Instead, focus on a long-term strategy of winning over the course of the season, winning the championship, and continuing to have winning seasons and win championships.

CHAPTER 7

Human Capital & Relationship Capital

For the Aligned Capital Strategy™ to work, you need to optimize your Human & Relationship Capital. In this chapter, we'll explore how to build a team of financial professionals who can help you Get Wealthy For Sure™.

What level are your coaches playing at?

I played sports in high school and college, and I had great coaches at every level. My college coach wasn't better than my high school coach. They were each great at coaching at a certain level. My high school coach knew how to coach high school kids to excel at that level and get chosen for college teams. My college coach knew how to coach players to excel at college sports. Meanwhile, an Olympic coach knows how to train players for the Olympics.

If my high school coach and an Olympic coach traded places for a week, they might not get the best results. Sure, the Olympic coach has more prestige, but he may not know how to work with young, non-professional players who are honing their skills for the first time. Meanwhile, my high school coach may not be able to help Olympic athletes with more advanced techniques. One isn't better than the other. They're just experts at different levels.

It works the same in business. The financial professionals who helped you thrive when you were just launching your business were great for that stage of your business. But now that you've grown, you may be playing at a level that these professionals don't have much experience with. As your business changes, you need to fill your financial team with professionals who are experts at working with business owners on your "level." For example, if your CPA is telling you that the best strategy for minimizing your taxes is maximizing your qualified plans, he's not playing at your level.

Not only do all of these professionals need to be playing on your level, but they need to be playing on the same level as each other so you have an aligned, unified team. If you have a high-quality life insurance professional who only works with business owners of your caliber and a generic banker, it would be like having Tom Brady as your quarterback with a high schooler playing defense.

Who should be on your team?

The people you need to protect you and position you for success are:

- A tax strategist & CPA
- A tax attorney
- An accountant
- A business attorney
- A bookkeeper
- An asset protection person
- An estate planning attorney
- A captive insurance attorney
- A life insurance agent
- A property and casualty insurance agent
- A business insurance agent
- A medical insurance agent
- A Registered Investment Advisor (RIA) & Fiduciary
- A real estate professional
- A stockbroker
- A mortgage broker
- A banker
- A mentor
- A life coach

All of these professionals are an investment... Yet too many business owners view them as an expense and try to cut corners. This comes from a scarcity mindset. If you consider the amount of money these professionals can save you over a lifetime, you'll understand that they're well worth the investment. And the return on investment is so much more than money... What if you get sued and a creditor takes your assets? What if you pass away without a properly set up estate plan and the assets you worked a lifetime to build pass to the government? Working with trusted, high-quality experts throughout your life helps you prevent these catastrophic scenarios.

Not All Advisors Are the Same

There are several different types of life insurance advisors, and they definitely aren't created equal.

First, we have advisors who sell retail life insurance to the general public. They sell straightforward, cookie-cutter insurance policies off the shelf. There's nothing wrong with this–people need insurance, and they sell it. But if you're looking for a more complex, specialized service, these advisors won't be able to help you.

Then you have life insurance advisors who are riding the hype of social media or network marketing. This is your TikTok life insurance advisor who creates catchy videos… But none of his followers know that he's just a bartender who sells life insurance as a side hustle. Nothing against bartenders. I have bartended in my life and loved it, but if you're a high-net-worth individual trying to execute a complex strategy, you need an advisor who works in life insurance full-time.

There are life insurance advisors who specialize in serving affluent markets. They'll be familiar with sophisticated, advanced life insurance strategies such as high cash-value policy designs. These advisors don't sell "cookie cutter" or "off the shelf" policies. Instead, they customize policies to achieve the goals of the specific client.

Some life insurance advisors specialize in specific strategies. The challenge with specialists is that you have to find one who specializes in the strategy you're looking for. Otherwise, they may not know how to execute it because they're only trained in one niche. For example, in my peer group, I know an advisor who specializes in bank-owned life insurance (BOLI), another advisor who specializes in corporate-owned life insurance (COLI), and a third advisor who specializes in setting up executive compensation packages for high-level CEOs. These advisors are fantastic, high-quality professionals, but they wouldn't be able to help you with anything outside of their niche. Only go to a specialist when you need their specialty—you wouldn't ask a heart surgeon to perform brain surgery.

Even if you find the right advisor, someone who practices full-time, specializes in what you're looking for, and works with high-net-worth clients, you need to find someone who practices what they preach.

If your goal is to get healthy and fit, you're not going to work with a dietician who eats McDonald's every day or a personal trainer who's out of shape. When you seek out mentors to help you achieve a goal, you want to work with people who have already achieved your goal.

The person giving you financial advice shouldn't be broke. If you want to execute the Aligned Capital Strategy™, you want to work with someone who has been successfully leveraging that strategy for years. My team and I all use this strategy in our personal lives, which allows us to see what works and optimize the strategy.

As a business owner, you should take financial advice from another business owner, not a financial salesperson.

If a professional doesn't use the strategy they sell, it's a red flag. Why would someone proclaim a strategy to be the greatest thing ever in a sales meeting with a client…and then not use it themselves? It's like a chef who doesn't eat their own cooking because they don't like the taste.

But when you work with an advisor who has used this strategy for years, you'll be able to harness their expertise to Get Wealthy For Sure™.

Don't Forget Your Family

The most important part of your team is your family.

Your assets are yourself, your family, and your business. Your family is the reason you're doing all of this, and the business is your tool to create wealth and security for your family.

Through this strategy, you're going to make sure your family is protected and set up a family bank.

Personally, I've set up a family bank using this life insurance strategy. This has provided my family and me with clarity, certainty, predictability, and protection. We're not reliant on third parties to get financing when we want to invest in assets or grow the business.

And, if executed correctly, this strategy can have an exponential impact on your family, passing through the generations for years to come.

Tip: Pay Your Kids

Want to fund your children's life insurance policies? Employ your kids in your business and pay them up to the legal limit without incurring taxes. In 2024, you can pay your kids up to $14,600 without them incurring any taxes. Your kids can help you with tasks like filing paperwork, taking out the trash, and cleaning the office. Your business can write off the amount you pay them on taxes, and you can use this money to fund your children's life insurance policies. Meanwhile, your children can learn about responsibility and gain their first work experience in the family business—it's a win-win situation." Please consult with your tax professionals when exploring this strategy.

CHAPTER 8

Capital Creation & Financial Capital

Let me introduce you to an equation:

Intellectual Capital + Relationship Capital = Financial Capital

You are the most important asset in your business. Your knowledge, wisdom, skills, and unique abilities make up your intellectual capital. You can increase the value of this intellectual capital by learning, growing, and expanding your skills.

Just as important is your relationship capital. This is made up of relationships you have with your family, your advisors, your team, and people in your network. You can increase the value of this capital by deepening your current relationships and building new relationships.

When you combine your intellectual capital and your relationship capital, it creates financial capital.

Business owners who don't understand this equation might focus squarely on financial capital. Yet they may find themselves stagnating and struggling to get results because they've missed what drives financial capital.

But if you focus on growing your intellectual capital and relationship capital, financial capital will come as a result.

Don't Take Your Eye Off the Ball

If you now see the whole picture and want to create your own banking system, don't lose focus on the main driver of this bank, which is creating financial capital by growing your business—and creating this financial capital through your intellectual and relationship capital.

Your income is what will make your own banking system strategy work. Continue to grow that so you can magnify the impact of this strategy.

When you have a strategy that protects you, your family, and your business, you will have clarity, confidence, and a strong foundation that will allow you to grow your business.

Knowing that your assets will be protected if you die or become disabled, you're free to focus on doing what you do best–growing your business through growing your intellectual and relationship capital so you can have more financial capital to fund your banking system.

CHAPTER 9

Capital Capture

Nelson Nash, creator of the infinite banking concept, who wrote *Becoming Your Own Banker*, told me this story:

The world is mostly made up of water.

The surface of the Earth is covered with oceans that are connected to each other, and there are rivers that are all connected to the ocean. Under the land, you have underground water.

The Sun heats up the Earth, clouds start to form, and the clouds get heavier and heavier until they eventually break, and then water returns to Earth in the form of rain.

Where does it end up? It goes back into the oceans or rivers, which are all connected, or it seeps into the land to the underground water, which is connected to the rivers and the oceans.

It's all connected. And this system repeats over and over.

What does this have to do with money?

Think about the banking system. The commercial banks have this all figured out. Money resides in the banking system. The famous bank robber Willie Sutton, on being asked why he robs banks, said, "Because that's where the money is."

So there's money in the banks, but money always leaves the banks. It could leave through loans or through lines of credit payments, but it always comes back to the banking system.

If somebody were to apply for a mortgage from a bank to buy a house, the bank gives them a check to take to the closing. They hand over the check at the closing table and get the keys to the house. What happens to the check? The check is then deposited into the seller's bank account. The money returns to the bank...

If you went to a restaurant for dinner tonight, you would pay for the meal, and the server would run your credit or debit card into the restaurant's merchant account. Money goes from your credit card or bank account into the restaurant's merchant account. The restaurant owner later uses that money to pay the waitstaff, the cooks, and the dishwashers. Where does the money end up? In all of their bank accounts.

Like water leaving the Earth and returning to it, money constantly leaves and returns to the banking system.

Banks have figured out how to capture capital in their system and never lose it.

How can we use this exact same concept in our own lives for our personal economy, our business economy, and our investing economy?

We can set up pools of capital in our own personal, business, and investing economy, and these pools of capital will do the exact same thing for us.

You can fund your policy with capital that comes into your economy, capturing it inside the policy. Once you put it there, it never leaves. You can establish a line of credit against it, so you become your own source of financing. You can use it to finance the growth of your business, which generates more capital. That capital is then used to pay down the line of credit, and you continue to fund the policy premiums. You've established this pool of capital in your own personal business and investing economy that's now capturing the value of what you produce and create in the marketplace. As you continue, it snowballs.

The Banking Model

What does a bank do?

It takes in deposits. Why would people deposit money in a bank? In exchange for keeping your money in the bank, you get benefits such as using a debit card, being able to transfer money, paying bills electronically, and earning a decent return.

But deposits are just the front end of the business model. Everyone knows the money is made on the back end...

The back end of the banking model is lending. The bank stores all of the capital that customers have deposited into it, and they lend this capital to other customers. They may issue credit cards, personal loans, automobile loans, business credit cards, business lines of credit, mortgages, commercial mortgages, and more.

Let's say you put $10,000 into the bank, and they pay you 1% ($100). On the bank end, they loan out that $10,000 at 10%, so they make $1,000.

Someone might look at that and say, "Nice, they made a 9% spread."

Not quite... There's one thing missing. You deposited $10,000 into the bank account on the front end. They lent that money out on the back end. The only money the bank had in the transaction was the $100 they paid you. The bank didn't make a 9% spread... It made a 900% spread.

THE BANKING BUSINESS MODEL

DEPOSIT **BANK** LENDING

1% $10,000 **10%**

$100 **9%?** $1000

$900 PROFIT

900%

Who benefits in this model? The banker and the owners of the bank.

But what if you could set up your own banking system that you could benefit from?

In life, you finance everything you buy. Whether you pay cash for it, leverage credit for it, or rent it, you're financing everything. Your banking system is at the forefront of letting you be the owner of the system that now finances your family, your business, and other investments.

Your need for financing during your lifetime exceeds your need for life insurance protection. Yes, you have a death benefit in your policy, but the real purpose of your policy is the banking system.

The average American pays 34.5% in interest and 30% in taxes (income, real estate, sales). So 64.5%, which is basically two-thirds of the income of the average American, goes to banks and the government.

This banking system is going to help you create your own pool of capital so you can recapture the interest that's paid out to third parties. (And later in the book, I'll show you a tax strategy to recapture the money you lose to taxes).

Maximize Your Banking System

There are four types of people in the banking system:

1. Consumers, who are people that borrow to spend
2. Producers, who are people, such as business owners, who borrow capital to create value and are the biggest depositors in banks
3. The banker, who finances both the consumers and producers
4. The bank owner, who owns the system

When you create your banking system, you take on the role of the bank owner.

You can follow the banking model with your life insurance policy. On the front end, you pay premiums and deposit money into your banking system. On the back end, you can lend yourself money when you need it for opportunities or emergencies.

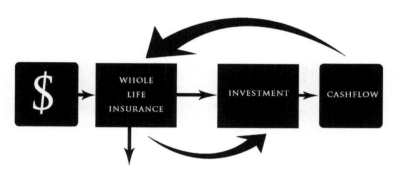

EARN DIVIDENDS

With this system, you can plug cashflow leaks and lower the cost of your insurance. You can opt for less expensive insurance with the highest deductibles and use your family bank to cover deductibles should you have an emergency.

When I bought insurance for my family, the gold plan was $3,500 a month for four people, while the bronze plan was $1,000 a month. We opted for the bronze plan and deposited the $2,500 we saved into our family bank. If an emergency happens, we can use that money to pay the deductibles. When I had an emergency appendix surgery, I used a policy loan to pay my high deductible of $17,000. But if no emergency happens, that money stays in the banking system and compounds.

Just as a leak in a pool allows water to escape, a leak in your banking system allows capital to leak out, making your system inefficient. Insurance deductibles are one of the most common leaks people have. If you have a family bank, you don't need insurance for potential fender benders or hospital visits.

My philosophy is that insurance is not there for fender benders or replacing broken windshields. It's for catastrophic events. Insurance exists so that you don't suffer a loss in your financial situation if a catastrophe occurs. It puts you back in the situation you were in before the catastrophe. For example, if you are in a major accident and your car is totaled, insurance puts you back in the situation you were in before the accident—you have a car. Meanwhile, if you have a fender bender, rather than paying for insurance, you may be better off writing a $500 check to get the car repaired.

When you have a banking system, you already have the ability to cover emergencies through policy loans. Meanwhile, with insurance, there's always the possibility that you never need to utilize it, in which case that money has leaked out of your bank for no reason.

Using a banking system as insurance rather than purchasing other policies saves our clients thousands of dollars per year.

That $2,500 a month I saved amounts to $30,000 a year. Over a period of just five years, that's $150,000 saved.

On the front end of your banking system, you make deposits that build up equity and cash value in your banking system. With every deposit, your family's net worth increases, guaranteed. There's no other vehicle I know of that can do that.

Yet you also have access to the lending arm of your bank. You can use policy loans to pay for things you're going to pay for anyway, allowing your capital to compound in the bank. You can give yourself personal loans, college loans, auto loans, business loans, and mortgages. You can buy a house, buy a car, send your kids to college, and invest in rental properties all with loans from your policy. You can take any type of loan you would ordinarily take from a bank, except the difference is that you're now making payments to your own banking system. As you are paying your own banking system back, you have a revolving line of credit. You don't have to pay off all of the loans from your system to get access to another loan from the system.

Borrowing from your own banking system allows you to patch another leak in your pool, which is outstanding loans to banks or credit card companies, with astronomical interest rates that eat away at your capital. When you establish your family bank, you can pay off inefficient loans to third parties with your banking system and then repay your own system. As Ben Franklin once said, "Beware of little expenses–a small leak will sink a great ship."

It may take time for you to build up your bank, but you have certainty that whatever you put in your bank will be there years from now. When you establish your own pool of capital and begin to fill it, it feels like building a swimming pool and filling it with water, thinking, "I can swim in that pool soon!"

You're eager to begin your journey with the Aligned Capital Strategy™, but you may be wondering, "Where do I find the money to start my policy?"

When you plug the leaks in your personal, business, and investment economy, you'll recoup thousands of dollars per year that can be used to fund and fuel your life insurance policy.

You can stop contributing to your 401(k) (or only contribute up to what your company will match) or Roth IRA (or only contribute up to the max). In some cases, it may make sense to cash out of qualified plans and use the capital to fund a life insurance policy.

Any excess capital such as savings, tax refunds, inheritance, or proceeds from selling a business or real estate, can be used to fuel your system.

Beyond these sources of capital, you can also consider making small lifestyle changes to have more capital available to fund your policy.

Now, when I say lifestyle changes, I don't mean adopt a scarcity mindset and pinch pennies.

Instead, I encourage you to think like a wealthy person and view all of your expenses as investments.

For example, a gym membership isn't an expense. It's an investment in your health and longevity. A vacation with your family isn't an expense. It's an investment in your happiness and relationships with your loved ones. Even your electricity bill is an investment... It enables you to be productive.

But some things you purchase are expenses, not investments. Anything frivolous that doesn't make you happy or help you move toward your goals is an expense. For example, buying luxury products just to impress other people is an expense.

Evaluate all of the things you spend money on and ask yourself, "Does this add value to my life or take value away?" Eliminate spending on anything that has no value and consider everything else an investment. Invest the money you've reclaimed from frivolous expenses into your life insurance policy.

Another way to find capital is to refinance from a 15-year mortgage to a 30-year mortgage. This is the opposite of advice you've probably heard from financial influencers. Believe it or not, a 30-year mortgage is the most optimized mortgage. If you take out a 15-year mortgage, your payments are higher, which means you're paying the bank back quicker in money that's worth more today than it will be worth in the future. Also, you're increasing your risk as the buyer of that property. The more equity you have in a property, the less risk it is for the bank and the more risk it is for you.

⌐ But if you lock in low-interest rates for a 30-year fixed loan, you free up more cash today–and your cash is worth more today than it will ever be due to inflation. You can then put that cash in your own banking system so it can compound.

You may be reading this thinking, "What have I done? I've paid off my mortgage, and my money is just sitting there doing nothing." You can get a home equity line of credit and then access that equity to put your capital to work in a policy.

With the Aligned Capital Strategy™, you can have the best of both worlds: you know you have the capital to pay off your 30-year mortgage at any time, yet by not paying off the mortgage, you have your capital growing tax-free, giving you an opportunity fund to make investments and grow your wealth. This is an ideal situation if one spouse is more conservative with money while the other spouse is more aggressive with it.

Using a combination of these approaches, you can patch up the leaks in your financial system, pool your capital into your life insurance policy, and Get Wealthy For Sure™.

CHAPTER 10

Cashflow Creation

Now that you have your banking system set up, you can use it to fund the growth of your business—and so much more.

Earlier in the book, we covered the equation:

Intellectual Capital + Relationship Capital = Financial Capital

When you combine intellectual and relationship capital to create financial capital, you then put your financial capital in your vehicle and use your banking system to exponentially grow your business.

In this chapter, we'll cover ways that you as a business owner can use this system for growth.

Financing Equipment

John owns a manufacturing business and needs to buy a piece of equipment that costs $50,000. He takes a policy loan from his banking system at a 6% interest rate to finance the equipment purchase. He doesn't need to go through any credit checks or wait for approvals, and he's able to get the funds within 48 to 72 hours.

Instead of paying the loan back directly, John decides to issue a note to his business wherein the business will pay the loan back in five years at a 10% interest rate. This arrangement creates an internal revenue stream for John that generates income for him that gets put back in the banking system. The interest that is paid on the loan for the business is tax deductible. He can also benefit from the tax code to depreciate the equipment.

Over five years, in total, John pays $15,000 in interest on the policy loan at a 6% interest rate. The business paid John a total of $25,000 interest at 10%. John profited $10,000 from the spread of 4% between interest paid on the policy loan and interest received on the business loan. At the same time, that $50,000 was growing tax-free in the policy.

Down Market Opportunities & Marketing Investments

A client in the marketing business took a $100,000 policy loan from his banking system and used it to run a Facebook and Instagram campaign that generated 10,000 leads.

The best part of this story is that it happened the first week that COVID hit… His competitors were frozen with fear, unsure of their futures, and unwilling to pour capital into marketing, so ads dried up. Meanwhile, this client took advantage of the low cost of ads that week and the low volume of ads from his competitors to run a massive campaign. He closed 500 clients for a consulting offer of $2,500... His $100,000 investment generated $1.25 million in revenue.

When you have a banking system, you can capture opportunities in a down market, when your competitors are cash short and unable to play the game. While your competitors are struggling, you can continue to grow.

And let's be real... A traditional bank would never give you a loan for a marketing campaign, regardless of how good your business plan is, even in a great market. Marketing campaigns are essential to generating more revenue by capturing clients, and a banking system allows you to use policy loans to invest in marketing and accelerate your business growth. You get to bet on yourself.

Investing In Other Assets

We all remember watching on the news as Lehman Brothers employees walked out of the building with boxes when the company crashed in 2008. And we all remember what happened after that... The financial markets around the world collapsed... There was a massive real estate collapse in the United States...

At the time, real estate investors believed you should have as many HELOCs as possible on all of your properties. The banks were loving it... Until they didn't. After the economic collapse, what do you think the banks did to all of the

HELOCs that investors had on all of their properties during the great financial crisis? They started to pull them and say, "Sorry, the product is no longer available."

But if you had access to capital at this time, when the average housing market was down 40%, you could buy real estate at a massive discount.

Who had access to capital at that time? Real estate investors that had dividend-paying, whole life insurance policies with mutual life insurance carriers set up as a personal banking system. These people had guaranteed access to policy loans at a time when getting traditional loans was virtually impossible.

When you have your own banking system, you have capital available to invest in assets outside of your business, even at times when other investors are unable to get loans. You have the power to capture unique opportunities to build your wealth and continue to grow the capital in your personal bank.

Preparation Over Prediction

All of the stories in this chapter demonstrate that if you are prepared, you can take advantage of opportunities and plug cashflow leaks when needed.

But since we can't predict the future, we have to lay the groundwork of preparation before the next opportunity or crisis arises.

You don't know what's coming–start preparing now.

CHAPTER 11

Capital Control, Taxes, Asset Protection, & Estate Planning

If a penny doubled every day for 30 days, it would compound to $5,368,709.12... That's just the penny doubling...

But what if with every double, you had to pay 30% in taxes?

At the end of 30 days, you would only have $81,934.66 left.

Due to taxes, you lost $5,286,774.46.

Whether you know it or not, due to taxes, you're on the wrong side of a compound interest equation.

You have to account for taxes in a financial plan–if you don't, taxes could destroy you.

To control taxes, you pay taxes on the seed, not the harvest. Since we can't predict what tax rates will be, deferring taxes to the "harvest" is a dangerous game.

But what do financial institutions and the government incentivize you to do? Pay taxes on the harvest. Remember, Uncle Sam's not your real uncle. These institutions benefit from you paying more in taxes.

You're Not Playing the Game

If you do not deal with Wall Street and Washington D.C. on your terms and keep them out of your pockets, you will never build the wealth you have the potential to build.

I'm going to say something that might make people mad: the tax code is 100% fair.

The tax code is a book thicker than the encyclopedia, and it's filled with ways you can legally reduce your taxes.

The tax code is fair—if you play the game.

The tax code rewards creators and producers. Employees and self-employed people pay the most in taxes, while business owners and investors pay the least. The government is incentivizing business owners, who create value in the marketplace through their products or services. Business owners take on risk so they can solve problems for consumers through what they create. Earning income through owning a business is one of the most tax-efficient types of income to earn.

The tax code also incentivizes you on where to position your capital. If you warehouse your capital inside a dividend-paying whole life insurance policy with a mutual insurance company, your capital grows tax-free. Why?

Life insurance is a bedrock of society. If someone in a community passes away, life insurance provides for the family of the deceased. Without life insurance, if the breadwinner of a family died, the surviving family members would need financial support from the government or would need to be helped out by extended family and friends. In a world without life insurance, every death would turn into a financial catastrophe that would cause grieving families to lose their lifestyles. Life insurance benefits society, so the government encourages people to have life insurance policies by making them tax-free savings vehicles.

After you've earned tax-efficient income and practiced tax-efficient capital warehousing, the third step to winning the tax game is tax-efficient deployment of capital. The tax code incentivizes specific investment areas that benefit society.

For example, the tax code incentivizes you to reinvest in your business. When you grow your business, you're creating more jobs and adding more value to the marketplace. As your business grows, you'll need more equipment from vendors, which helps those businesses grow as well. Growing your business stimulates the economy, so it's tax-efficient to reinvest in your business.

The government doesn't want to be a landlord, so real estate investing is also incentivized. The government needs real estate investors to provide affordable housing for people, so real estate is a tax-efficient investment.

Another incentivized investment area is energy, whether it's oil and gas or greener technologies.

To be tax efficient, you need to legally reduce your taxes by playing the tax game and pay taxes on the seed, not the harvest. The worst financial strategy on the planet is to defer taxes until a future date, like you do with qualified plans like 401k, 403Bs, and IRAs.

If you use the tax code as a rulebook, you can reduce your taxes so you can pay as little as possible. You should absolutely pay the taxes you owe… But that doesn't mean you have to leave Uncle Sam a tip.

After all, Uncle Sam is not your Uncle!

Capture Your Capital First

So, you've played the tax game.

You've earned tax-efficient income, stored it in a tax-efficient warehouse, and deployed it in an efficient way.

You've reduced your tax burden, but you still have to pay some amount in taxes. What now?

Before paying taxes, you're going to first capture that capital in your banking system and pay taxes through a policy loan.

Then, you can pay yourself back all at once or over a period of time.

Let's say a business owner takes $1 million in income per year from the business and pays $300,000 a year in taxes over a ten-year period. That's a $3 million cashflow leak…

Not to mention the opportunity cost of $3 million. Can you imagine what that $3 million could have grown to if it earned 3-4% tax-free?

I am getting nauseous just thinking about it.

But if you capture the capital before paying taxes to the government, you don't pay the opportunity cost of that leak because you can allow that capital to compound in the policy.

Protect Your Biggest Assets

In the United States, you don't have to do anything wrong to get sued. As a business owner, you probably know this.

But what's shocking is that 95% of lawsuits settle out of court… Business owners surrender to their creditors because they realize that they weren't as protected as they should have been and don't want to lose more money to legal fees. They thought they were bulletproof, but they weren't, and they lose money as a result.

When you have proper asset protection in place, you can flip this narrative: your creditors will drop the lawsuit before it goes to court because they realize they can't win anything from you.

However, there's always a chance that you'll be sued and need to go to court. A banking system allows you to have liquidity on hand to afford to put up a legal fight–and avoid settling out of court because you don't have cash on hand to fund a legal battle.

Estate Planning

 *"A good man leaves an inheritance for his children's children."*
                                    --Proverbs 13:22

Believe it or not, I run into people all the time who say, "When I die, I'm not leaving anything for anybody."

What these people don't understand is that inheritance doesn't have to come in the form of a check. A more impactful legacy is to give your heirs a system that allows them to tap into opportunities and grow the family wealth after you're gone.

The goal of estate planning is to protect, preserve, and expand the wealth of the family, contractually, for generations and generations to come. Plant the seeds of a tree that you will never sit beneath.

The Family Office Model, which has been used by wealthy families throughout history, from the Medicis to the Roth-schilds to the Sassoons to the Rockefellers, tells you how to adopt this philosophy. There are five components to this model:

1. Family legacy assets
2. The family legal and tax structures
3. The family bank
4. Family asset management
5. Family masterminds

Family legacy assets include a statement of purpose (which is like your family's Declaration of Independence), a family Constitution that covers your guiding principles and framework, and a family legacy library that includes videos, letters, photos, and more that you can leave for your descendants. Your family legacy assets allow you to share your values with future generations.

The family legal and tax structures provide the infrastructure to protect the assets, optimize transferring them through estate planning strategies throughout every generation, and reduce taxes legally.

The family bank finances the entire family, whether it be for personal, business, or investing matters. It is the mechanism that compounds the capital of the family tax-free forever.

The family asset management includes the active management of the family assets, making sure the family's assets are aligned at all times to ensure the wealth potential of the family. Assets such as income-generating businesses and real estate that are aligned with the family's wealth

DNA are actively managed with the asset management team, strategy, systems, vehicles, and processes.

The family masterminds are retreats in which the family gets aligned on the vision and goals of the family, the family guiding principles and values, and shares best practices.

These five components allow you to protect, preserve, and expand your family's wealth across generations–to be like the Rockefellers, not the Vanderbilts.

When you ask a poor or middle-class family how much life insurance they want to buy, they either tell you that they want to self-insure (which means having no insurance) or they will buy term and invest the rest.

But when you ask a wealthy family how much life insurance they want to buy, their answer is, "As much as they will sell me."

Before you read this book, you probably thought they were crazy. But now, do you start to understand why the family bank is foundational in protecting, preserving, and expanding the wealth of the family? With each and every generation, when life insurance is maxed out, there's a windfall of millions of dollars from one generation to another as family members pass away. Family offices call this the "waterfall strategy." This is what families like the Rockefellers do to ensure that the wealth built by one generation is multiplied when it is transferred from one generation to the next and isn't lost by the next generation.

You do not have to be a Rockefeller to protect, preserve, and expand your family's wealth like a Rockefeller.

CHAPTER 12

You Can Do It All Right and Have It All Go Wrong

In an ideal world, you build your own banking system, and this vehicle compounds for generations, exponentially growing your family's wealth and freeing your descendants from reliance on traditional banks. But for this to work, your family matters…

We've already covered how the Vanderbilts were once one of the richest families in America until successive generations squandered their wealth. If your family members are misaligned with the long-term vision of the family, they can make decisions that erode the family wealth you've built.

Take the stereotypical "trust fund baby" who coasts off their family's wealth without creating value, wasting the family money on luxury items and approaching life with a spoiled, entitled attitude. To prevent your descendants from adopting this mindset, you need to instill them with values around finances.

Get It Right

Remember, there are a lot of pieces that need to be done right for the Aligned Capital Strategy™ to work so that you can Get Wealthy For Sure™.

You need:

- A Team
- A Strategy
- A System
- Vehicles
- Processes

Without all of these pieces in place, the system won't work.

If your team is fragmented and isn't at the same level of talent–or doesn't specialize in this strategy–you won't have the expert guidance needed to execute this strategy.

If you don't have a cohesive strategy and instead try various strategies that aren't aligned with each other, you don't really have a strategy. You're hoping, not planning.

Without a clear strategy, it's impossible to have an effective system. This usually leads to having a variety of vehicles that you don't truly understand and hoping one of them works out. And without all of these four pieces, your processes will be sporadic and disorganized. How can you execute an effective process if you don't understand the vehicles you have, what they do in your system, and what your overall strategy is?

Many business owners get lost chasing shiny objects or implementing the hot new investment vehicle of the month. Because their team and strategy aren't in alignment, nobody stops them from falling down the rabbit hole.

In the end, without these 5 components, you don't get predictable results. To return to our mountain analogy, you have no idea what will happen when you reach the summit.

A proper strategy that aligns a team, system, vehicle, and processes toward your goals will give you predictable results. You will know for certain that you'll get the outcome you want.

If you don't have these 5 components aligned yet, it's okay. It's not too late to move from where you are to where you want to be.

CHAPTER 13

Get Wealthy For Sure™

When you implement the strategy we've discussed in this book, you will gain:

1. **Clarity**

    You now have clarity because all of your assets are aligned to multiply wealth.

    Clarity turns into confidence. You now have the confidence that you have the right foundation. You have a team, strategy, systems, a vehicle, and processes that are all aligned and will get you where you want to go. This gives you time to focus on what you do best—growing your business. No more sleepless nights...

2. **Certainty**

    You know and understand the strategy that you control. You have access to capital for both business investments and emergencies... No need to jump through hoops with the bank when you need cash. You know how much capital you will have in your banking system at any given point in time, even into the future.

3. **Predictability**

There is no guessing with this system. A dividend-paying whole life insurance policy with a mutual carrier is the one vehicle that's going to do what you want it to do, when you want it to. You know exactly what will happen, even when you're no longer around to see it. You now have a rock-solid financial foundation.

4. **Tax-Free**

You've taken control of your taxes. You can now recapture all of the capital that would normally leak out of your system when you pay taxes. You now have a proper tax strategy that is based on tax-free growth, not tax deferral. With this strategy, you can pay taxes on the seed today instead of hoping that tax rates will be favorable in the future.

5. **Family Contingency Planning in Place**

Your family is one of your greatest assets. Now, you have the certainty, clarity, and predictability that your family will be protected. You have protected your future ability to produce and create.

6. **Business Contingency Planning In Place**

Your business, which drives the cashflow to fund the system, is protected. You have a contingency and succession plan in place that will enable your business to weather any storm. You have protected the future of your business through business contingency.

7. **Assets Are Protected**
   You are your #1 asset. You, your family, and your business are protected by the Aligned Capital Strategy™.

What will your life look like one year from today?

Will you be wealthier?

Will you be less stressed about money?

Will you be paying less in taxes?

Will you have more certainty about the future of your family, business, and investments?

Will you be living and building a life you love?

Tony Robbins once said, "It is in your moments of decision that your destiny is shaped."

Now, you have one decision before you. Will you take action towards getting wealthy for sure, or will you stick with the status quo?

If you're ready to take the next step toward being the master of your financial destiny, you have three options.

1. **Do Nothing.** Sorry for wasting your time with this book!

2. **Watch our video presentation** to learn more. https://getwealthyforsure.com/

3. **Book a strategy session.** Complete our intake form to explore options for you, your family, and your business. https://producerswealth.com/become-a-client/

"Even if you are on the right track, you'll get run over if you just sit there."

–Will Rogers

ABOUT THE AUTHOR

 M.C. Laubscher is a husband, father, business owner, investor, podcaster, and author.

As one of the leading voices in alternative wealth strategies and alternative asset investing, M.C.'s passion is helping business owners achieve more freedom and sovereignty and live and leave a legacy for their families.

M.C. is the founder of Producers Wealth, a firm helping business owners in all 50 states in the United States implement and execute advanced alternative wealth strategies.

Producers Wealth's mission is to elevate the financial well-being of business owners and their families. Producers Wealth assists business owners in the United States in all 50 states to implement and execute the #1 financial strategy for business owners to predictably multiply their wealth.

M.C. is the creator & host of the top-rated business and investing podcasts Cashflow Ninja, Cashflow Investing Secrets, and Cashflow Ninja Banking.

The Cashflow Ninja podcast has been featured by Entrepreneur Magazine as one of the top 48 podcasts for entrepreneurs and is regularly featured as one of the top 100 business podcasts by Apple Podcasts and Spotify. It has been downloaded millions of times in over 180 countries.

M.C. is a best-selling author and has written The 21 Best Cashflow Niches™, The 21 Most Unique Cashflow Niches™, The 21 Best Cash Growth Niches™ and Get Wealthy for Sure™.

M.C. is a member of the Forbes Finance Council and The Million Dollar Round Table, a peer group for the top 1% of financial professionals worldwide. He is regularly featured on business and investing podcasts and is a sought-after speaker at business and investing conferences.

Made in the USA
Middletown, DE
08 July 2024